IF THE WAR
GOES ON . . .

If the War Goes On . . .

REFLECTIONS ON WAR AND POLITICS

HERMANN HESSE

TRANSLATED BY RALPH MANHEIM

Farrar, Straus and Giroux

NEW YORK

Dedicated to the memory

of my dear friend

Romain Rolland

Contents

IF THE WAR
GOES ON . . .

Foreword to the 1946 Edition

COMPILING THIS BOOK has not been a happy task for the author. It has not awakened pleasant memories or recalled welcome images. On the contrary, every single article reminded me painfully of times of suffering, struggle, and loneliness, times in which I was beset by enmity and incomprehension and bitterly cut off from pleasurable ideals and pleasant habits. In order to alleviate these ugly shadows, which have only deepened in recent years, with a note of beauty and light, I have recalled the one beautiful and enduring thing that came to me through those struggles and torments, by dedicating this book to a noble and beloved friend. I have forgotten much of what happened in those depressing days in 1914 when the first of these articles was written, but not the day on which a note from Romain Rolland brought me, along with an announcement of his forthcoming book, a sympathetic reaction—the only one I received at the time—to my article. I now had a like-minded companion, one who like myself was alert to the bloody absurdity of the war and the war psychosis and rebelled against it, and this companion was not an unknown quantity but the man I esteemed as the author of the first volumes of *Jean Christophe* (no more of his work was known to me at the time), a man far superior to me in political schooling and

(3

awareness. We remained friends until his death. The geographical distance between us as well as the divergent cultures and habits of thought in which we had grown to manhood made it impossible for me to become his disciple or to learn much from him in political matters. But that was not the essential. I had come to politics very late, when I was almost forty, jolted awake by the gruesome reality of the war and profoundly horrified at the ease with which my colleagues and friends had enlisted in the service of Moloch. Already a few friends had turned away from me and I had incurred the first of those attacks, threats, and insults which in so-called heroic times conformists never fail to heap upon a man who walks alone. It was by no means certain whether I would come through or be destroyed by the conflict that transformed my hitherto rather happy and undeservedly successful life into a hell. In that situation it was a great thing, a joy and a salvation, to learn that in France, in the "enemy" camp, there was a man whose conscience would not let him keep silent or participate in the prevailing orgies of hatred and morbid nationalism. Neither during the war years nor afterward did I actually discuss politics with Rolland; yet I doubt that I could have lived through those years without the warmth of his friendship. How then could I fail to think of him now?

A few words about the genesis of the present book: most of the articles connected with the war of 1914–1918 appeared in the *Neue Zürcher Nachrichten.* At that time (and until 1923) I was still a German citizen. Since then I have never been fully forgiven in Germany for having once taken a critical attitude toward patriotism and militarism. Though immediately after the lost war, as again today, a certain section of the German population felt very much drawn to pacifism and internationalism and occasionally echoed my ideas, I remained an object of distrust. Long before the first victories of National Socialism, I was regarded by official Germany as a suspicious and essentially undesirable character, worthy at best to be tolerated. In the period of its omnipotence, Hitler's party gleefully avenged itself on my books, my name, and my unfortunate Berlin publisher.

A glance at the table of contents will show that I wrote "political" or timely articles only in certain years. But from this it should not be inferred that I relapsed into sleep in between, and turned my back on current affairs. To my own great regret, this has been impossible for me since my first cruel awakening in the First World War. Anyone who looks into my life work as a whole will soon notice that even in the years when I wrote nothing on current affairs the thought of the hell smoldering beneath our feet, the sense of impending catastrophe and war, never left me. From *Steppenwolf*, which was in part a cry of anguished warning against the approaching war and which was attacked and ridiculed as such, down to *The Glass Bead Game* with its world of images seemingly so far removed from current realities, the reader will encounter this feeling time and time again, and the same tone may be heard repeatedly in the poems.

When I call my articles "political," it is always in quotes, for there is nothing political about them but the atmosphere in which they came into being. In all other respects they are the opposite of political, because in each one of these essays I strive to guide the reader not into the world theater with its political problems but into his innermost being, before the judgment seat of his very personal conscience. In this I am at odds with the political thinkers of all trends, and I shall always, incorrigibly, recognize in man, in the individual man and his soul, the existence of realms to which political impulses and forms do not extend. I am an individualist and I regard the Christian veneration for every human soul as what is best and most holy in Christianity. It may be that in this I partake of a world that is already half extinct, that we are witnessing the emergence of a collective man without individual soul, who will do away with the entire religious and individualistic tradition of mankind. To desire or fear such an eventuality is not my concern. I have always been impelled to serve the gods whom I felt to be living and helpful, and I have tried to do so even when I was certain to be answered with hostility or laughter. The path I was obliged to take between the demands of the world and those of my own soul was not pleasant or easy, I hope I shall not have to travel it again, for it ends in grief and bitter disappointments. But I can say without regret that since my first awakening I have not, like most of my colleagues and critics, been capable of learning a new lesson and rallying to a different flag every few years.

Since my first awakening thirty years ago my moral reaction to every great political event has always arisen instinctively and without effort on my part. My judgments have never wavered. Since I am an utterly unpolitical man, I myself have been astonished at the reliability of my reactions, and I have often pondered about the sources of this moral instinct, about the teachers and guides who, despite my lack of systematic concern with politics, so molded me that I have always been sure of my judgment and offered a more than average resistance to mass psychoses and psychological infections of every kind. A man ought to stand by what has educated, imprinted, and molded him, and so, after much consideration of the question, I must say: three strong influences, at work throughout my life, have made me what I am. These are the Christian and almost totally unnationalistic spirit of the home in which I grew up, the reading of the great Chinese thinkers, and last not least, the work of the one historian to whom I have ever been devoted in confidence, veneration, and grateful emulation: Jakob Burckhardt.

Montagnola, June 1946

O Freunde, nicht diese Töne!
September 1914

T HE NATIONS are at each other's throats; every day countless men are suffering and dying in terrible battles. In the midst of the sensational news from the front, I have recalled, as sometimes happens, a long-forgotten moment from my boyhood years. I was fourteen. One hot summer day I was sitting in a schoolroom in Stuttgart, taking the famous Swabian state examination. The subject of the essay we were to write was dictated to us: "What good and what bad aspects of human nature are aroused and developed by war?" What I wrote on the subject was based on no experience of any kind and accordingly the result was dismal; what I then as a boy understood about war, its virtues and burdens, had nothing in common with what I should call by these names today. But in connection with the daily events and that little reminiscence, I have lately thought a good deal about war, and since it has now become customary for men of the study and workshop to vent their opinions on the subject, I no longer hesitate to express mine. I am a German, my sympathies and aspirations belong to Germany; neverthe-

---

O Freunde, nicht diese Töne! (literally, "O Friends, not these tones!") has immediate associations for the cultivated German. These are the first words of the recitative, sung by the bass solo-ist, that introduces the choral setting of Schiller's *An die Freude* ("Ode to Joy") in the last movement of Beethoven's Ninth Symphony. [EDITOR'S NOTE]

less, what I wish to say relates not to war and politics but to the position and tasks of neutrals. By this I mean not the politically neutral nations but all those who as scientists, teachers, artists, and men of letters are engaged in the labors of peace and of humanity.

We have been struck lately by signs of a ruinous confusion among such neutrals. German patents have been suspended in Russia, German music is boycotted in France, the cultural productions of enemy nations are boycotted in Germany. Many German papers propose to carry no further translation, criticism, or even mention of works by Englishmen, Frenchmen, Russians, and Japanese. This is not a rumor but an actual decision that has already been put into practice.

A lovely Japanese fairy tale, a good French novel, faithfully and lovingly translated by a German before the war started, must now be passed over in silence. A magnificent gift, lovingly offered to our people, is rejected because a few Japanese ships are attacking Tsingtao. And if today I praise the work of an Italian, Turk, or Rumanian, I must be prepared for the possibility that some diplomat or journalist may transform these friendly nations into enemies before my article goes to press.

At the same time we see artists and scholars joining in the outcry against certain belligerent powers. As though today, when the world is on fire, such utterances could be of any value. As though an artist or man of letters, even the best and most famous of us, had any say in matters of war.

Others participate in the great events by carrying the war into their studies and writing bloodthirsty war songs or rabid articles fomenting hatred among nations. That perhaps is the worst of all. The men who are risking their lives every day at the front may be entitled to bitterness, to momentary anger and hatred; the same may be true of active politicians. But we writers, artists, and journalists —can it be our function to make things worse than they are? Is the situation not already ugly and deplorable enough?

Does it help France if all the artists in the world condemn the Germans for endangering a beautiful piece of architecture? Does it do Germany any good to stop reading English and French books? Is anything in the world made better, sounder, righter when a French author vilifies the enemy in the crudest terms and incites "his" army to bestial rage?

All these manifestations, from the unscrupulously invented "rumor" to the inflammatory article, from the boycotting of "enemy" art to the defamation of whole nations, have their source in a failure to think, in a mental laziness that is perfectly pardonable in a soldier at the front but ill becomes a thoughtful writer or artist. From this rebuke I exempt in advance all those who believed even before the war that the world stopped at our borders. I am not speaking of those who regarded all praise of French painting as an outrage and saw red when they heard a word of foreign origin; they are merely continuing to do what they did before. But all those others who were more or less consciously at work on the supranational edifice of human culture and have now suddenly decided to carry the war into the realm of the spirit— what they are doing is wrong and grotesquely unreasonable. They served humanity and believed in a supranational ideal of humanity as long as no crude reality conflicted with this ideal, as long as humanitarian thought and action seemed convenient and self-evident. But now that these same ideals involve hard work and danger, now that they have become a matter of life and death, they desert the cause and sing the tune that their neighbors want to hear.

These words, it goes without saying, are not directed against patriotic sentiment or love of country. I am the last man to forswear my country at a time like this, nor would it occur to me to deter a soldier from doing his duty. Since shooting is the order of the day, let there be shooting—not, however, for its own sake and not out of hatred for the execrable enemy but with a view to resuming as soon as possible a higher and better type of activity. Each day brings with it the destruction of much that all men of good will among the artists, scholars, travelers, translators, and journalists of all countries have striven for all their lives. This cannot be helped. But it is absurd and wrong that any man who ever, in a lucid hour, believed in the idea of humanity, in international thought, in an artistic beauty cutting across national boundaries, should now, frightened by the monstrous thing that has happened, throw down the banner and relegate what is best in him to the general ruin. Among our writers and men of letters there are, I believe, few if any whose present utterances, spoken or written in the anger of the moment, will be counted among their best work. Nor is there any serious writer who at heart prefers Körner's patriotic songs to the poems of the Goethe who held so conspicuously aloof from the War of Liberation.

Exactly, cry the super-patriots, we have always been suspicious of Goethe, he was never a patriot, he contaminated the German mind with the benign internationalism which has plagued us so long and appreciably weakened our German consciousness.

That is the crux of the question. Goethe was never wanting as a patriot, though he wrote no national anthems in 1813. But his devotion to humanity meant more to him than his devotion to the German people, which he knew and loved better than anyone else. He was a citizen and patriot in the international world of thought, of inner freedom, of intellectual conscience. In the moments of his best thinking, he saw the histories of nations no longer as separate, independent destinies but as subordinate parts of a total movement.

Perhaps such an attitude will be condemned as an ivory-tower intellectualism that should hold its tongue in a moment of serious danger—and yet it is the spirit in which the best German thinkers and writers have lived. There can be no better time than now to recall this spirit and the imperatives of justice, moderation, decency, and brotherhood it implies. Can we let things come to such a pass that only the bravest of Germans dare prefer a good English book to a bad German one? That the attitude of our military men, who treat an enemy prisoner with consideration, becomes a living reproach to our thinkers, who are no longer willing to respect and esteem the enemy even when he is peaceful and brings benefits? What is to happen after the war, in a period which even now inspires us with some misgiving, when travel and cultural exchange between nations will be at a standstill? And who can be expected to work toward a better state of affairs, toward mutual understanding—who, I say, if not those of us who are sitting here at our desks in the knowledge that our brothers are standing in the trenches? Honor be to every man who is risking his life amid shot and shell on the battlefield! Upon the rest of us, who love our country and do not despair of the future, it becomes incumbent to preserve an area of peace, to strike bridges, to look for ways, but not to lash out (with our pens!) and still further demolish the foundations of Europe's future.

One more word to those who are filled with despair by this war and believe that because there is a war all culture and humanity are dead. There has always been war, ever since the earliest human destinies known to us, and there was no reason on the eve of this one for the belief that war had been done away with. Such a belief was engendered only by the habit of a prolonged peace. There will be war until the majority of human beings are able to live in the Goethean realm of the human spirit. Wars will be with us for a long time, perhaps forever. Nevertheless, the elimination of war remains our noblest aim and the ultimate consequence of the Western, Christian ethic. A scientist searching for a way to combat a disease will not drop his work because a new epidemic has broken out. Much less will "peace on earth" and friendship among men ever cease to be our highest ideal. Human culture comes into being through the conversion of animal drives into more spiritual impulses, through the sense of shame, through imagination and knowledge. Though to this day no panegyrist of life has succeeded in escaping death, the conviction that life is worth living is the ultimate content and consolation of all art. Precisely this wretched World War must make us more keenly aware that love is higher than hate, understanding than anger, peace than war. Or what would be the good of it?

To a Cabinet Minister
August 1917

T HIS EVENING after a hard day's work I asked my
wife to play me a Beethoven sonata. With its
angelic voices the music recalled me from bustle and
worry to the real world, to the one reality which we possess, which gives us joy and torment, the reality in which
and for which we live.

Afterwards I read a few lines in the book containing the
Sermon on the Mount and the sublime, age-old, and fundamental words: "Thou shalt not kill!"

But I found no peace, I could neither go to bed nor continue reading. I was filled with anxiety and unrest, and
suddenly, Herr Minister, as I was searching my mind for
their cause, I remembered a few sentences from one of
your speeches that I read a few days ago.

Your speech was well constructed; otherwise, it was
not particularly original, significant, or provocative. Reduced to the essentials, it said roughly what government
officials have been saying in their speeches for a long
time: that, generally speaking, "we" long for nothing so
fervently as peace, as a new understanding among nations
and fruitful collaboration in building the future, that we
wish neither to enrich ourselves nor to satisfy homicidal
lusts—but that the "time for negotiations" is not yet at
hand and that for the present there is therefore no alter-

native but to go on bravely waging war. Just about every minister of any of the belligerent nations might have made such a speech, and probably will tomorrow or the day after.

If tonight your speech keeps me awake, although I have read many similar speeches with the same dreary conclusion and slept soundly afterwards, the fault, as I am now certain, lies with Beethoven's sonata and with that ancient book in which I afterwards read, that book which contains the wonderful commandments of Mount Sinai and the luminous words of the Saviour.

Beethoven's music and the words of the Bible told me exactly the same thing; they were water from the same spring, the only spring from which man derives good. And then suddenly, Herr Minister, it came to me that your speech and the speeches of your governing colleagues in both camps do not flow from that spring, that they lack what can make human words important and valuable. They lack love, they lack humanity.

Your speech shows a profound feeling of concern and responsibility for your people, its army, and its honor. But it shows no feeling for mankind. And, to put it bluntly, it implies hundreds of thousands more human sacrifices.

Perhaps you will call my reference to Beethoven sentimentality. I imagine, though, that you feel a certain respect for the Commandments and for the sayings of Jesus —at least in public. But if you believe in a single one of the ideals for which you are waging war, the freedom of nations, freedom of the seas, social progress, or the rights of small countries—if you truly, in your heart of hearts, believe in a single one of these generous ideals, you will have to recognize on rereading your speech that it does not serve that ideal or any other. It is not the expression and product of a faith, of any awareness of a human need, but, alas, the expression and product of a dilemma. An understandable dilemma, to be sure, for what could be more difficult at the present time than to acknowledge a certain disappointment with the course of the war and to start looking for the shortest way to peace?

But such a dilemma, even if it is shared by ten governments, cannot endure forever. Dilemmas are solved by necessities. One day it will become necessary for you and your enemy colleagues to face up to your dilemma and make decisions that will put an end to it.

The belligerents of both camps have long been disappointed with the course of the war. Regardless of who has won this battle or that battle, regardless of how much territory or how many prisoners have been taken or lost, the result has not been what one expects in a war. There has been no solution, no decision—and none is in sight.

You made your speech in order to hide this great dilemma from yourself and your people, in order to postpone vital decisions (which always call for sacrifices) —and other government officials make their speeches for the same reason. Which is understandable. It is easier for a revolutionary or even for a writer to see the human factor in a political situation and draw the proper inferences than for a responsible statesman. It is easier for one of us because he is under no obligation to feel personally responsible for the deep gloom that comes over a nation when it sees that it has not achieved its war aim and that many thousands of human lives and billions in wealth may well have been sacrificed in vain.

But that is not the only reason why it is harder for you to recognize the dilemma and make decisions that will put an end to the war. Another reason is that you hear too little music and read the Bible and the great authors too little.

You smile. Or perhaps you will say that you as a private citizen feel very close to Beethoven and to all that is noble and beautiful. And maybe you do. But my heartfelt wish is that one of these days, chancing to hear a piece of sublime music, you should suddenly recapture an awareness of those voices that well from a sacred spring. I wish that one of these days in a quiet moment you would read a parable of Jesus, a line of Goethe, or a saying of Lao-tzu.

That moment might be infinitely important to the world. You might find inner liberation. Your eyes and ears might suddenly be opened. For many years, Herr Minister, your eyes and ears have been attuned to theoretical aims rather than reality; they have long been accustomed —necessarily so!—to close themselves to much of what constitutes reality, to disregard it, to deny its existence. Do you know what I mean? Yes, you know. But perhaps the voice of a great poet, the voice of the Bible, the eternal voice of humanity that speaks clearly to us from art, would give you the power of true sight and hearing. What things you would see and hear! Nothing more about the labor shortage and the price of coal, nothing more about tonnages and alliances, loans, troop levies, and all the rest of what you have hitherto regarded as the sole reality. Instead, you would see the earth, our patient old earth, so littered with the dead and dying, so ravaged and shattered, so charred and desecrated. You would see soldiers lying for days in no-man's-land, unable with their mutilated hands to shoo the flies from their mortal wounds. You would hear the voices of the wounded, the screams of the mad, the accusing plaints of mothers and fathers, sweethearts and sisters, the people's cry of hunger.

If your ears should be opened once more to all these things that you have sedulously avoided hearing for months and years, then perhaps you would reexamine your aims, your ideals and theories, with a new mind and attempt to weigh their true worth against the misery of a single month, a single day, of war.

Oh, if this hour of music, this return to true reality, could somehow come your way! You would hear the voice of mankind, you would shut yourself up in your room and weep. And next day you would go out and do your duty toward mankind. You would sacrifice a few millions or billions in money, a trifling bit of prestige, and a thousand other things (all the things for which you are now prolonging the war), and, if need be, your minister's portfolio with them, and you would do what mankind, in untold fear and torment, is hoping and praying you will do. You would be the first among governing statesmen to condemn this wretched war, the first to tell his fellows what all feel secretly even now: that six months or even one month of war costs more than what anything it can achieve is worth.

If that were to happen, Herr Minister, your name would never be forgotten, your deed would stand higher in the eyes of mankind than the deeds of all those who have ever waged victorious wars.

If the War Goes on
Another Two Years
End of 1917

E VER SINCE I WAS A BOY I have been in the habit of
disappearing now and then, to restore myself by
immersion in other worlds. My friends would look for me
and after a time write me off as missing. When I finally
returned, it always amused me to hear what so-called
scientists had to say of my "absences," or twilight states.
Though I did nothing but what was second nature to me
and what sooner or later most people will be able to do,
those strange beings regarded me as a kind of freak; some
thought me possessed; others endowed me with miracu-
lous powers.

So now, once again, I vanished for a time. The present
had lost its charm for me after two or three years of war,
and I slipped away to breathe different air. I left the plane
on which we live and went to live on another plane. I
spent some time in remote regions of the past, raced
through nations and epochs without finding contentment,
observed the usual crucifixions, intrigues, and movements
of progress on earth, and then withdrew for a while into
the cosmic.

When I returned, it was 1920. I was disappointed to find

"If the War Goes on Another Two Years" was originally published
under the pseudonym Emil Sinclair, which Hesse used again
when he published *Demian* in 1919. [EDITOR'S NOTE]

the nations still battling one another with the same mindless obstinacy. A few frontiers had shifted; a few choice sites of older, higher cultures had been painstakingly destroyed; but, all in all, little had changed in the outward aspect of the earth.

Great progress had been made toward equality. In Europe at least, so I heard, all countries looked the same; even the difference between belligerent and neutral countries had virtually disappeared. Since the introduction of bombing from free balloons, which automatically dropped their bombs on the civilian population from an altitude of fifty to sixty thousand feet, national boundaries, though as closely guarded as ever, had become rather illusory. The dispersion of these bombs, dropped at random from the sky, was so great that the balloon commands were quite content if their explosive showers had spared their own country—how many landed on neutral or even allied territory had become a matter of indifference.

This was the only real progress the art of warfare had made; here at last the character of this war had found a clear expression. The world was divided into two parties which were trying to destroy each other because they both wanted the same thing, the liberation of the oppressed, the abolition of violence, and the establishment of a lasting peace. On both sides there was strong sentiment against any peace that might not last forever—if eternal peace was not to be had, both parties were resolutely committed to eternal war, and the insouciance with which the military balloons rained their blessings from prodigious heights on just and unjust alike reflected the inner spirit of this war to perfection. In other respects, however, it was being waged in the old way, with enormous but inadequate resources. The meager imagination of the military men and technicians had devised a few new instruments of destruction—but the visionary who had invented the automatic bomb-strewer balloon had been the last of his kind; for in the meantime the intellectuals, visionaries, poets, and dreamers had gradually lost interest in the war, and with only soldiers and technicians to count on, the military art made little progress. With marvelous perseverance, the armies stood and lay face to face. Though, what with the shortage of metals, military decorations had long consisted exclusively of paper, no diminution of bravery had anywhere been registered.

I found my house partly destroyed by aerial bombs, but still more or less fit to sleep in. However, it was cold and uncomfortable, the rubble on the floor and the mold on the walls were distressing, and I soon went out for a walk.

A great change had come over the city; there were no shops to be seen and the streets were lifeless. Before long, a man with a tin number pinned to his hat came up to me and asked me what I was doing. I said I was taking a walk. He: Have you got a permit? I didn't understand, an altercation ensued, and he ordered me to follow him to the nearest police station.

We came to a street where all the buildings had white signs bearing the names of offices followed by numbers and letters.

One sign read: "Unoccupied civilians 2487 B 4." We went in. The usual official premises, waiting rooms and corridors smelling of paper, damp clothing, and bureaucracy. After various inquiries I was taken to Room 72 and questioned.

An official looked me over. "Can't you stand at attention?" he asked me in a stern voice. "No," I said. "Why not?" he asked. "Because I never learned how," I said timidly.

"In any case," he said, "you were taking a walk without a permit. Do you admit that?"

"Yes," I said. "That seems to be true. I didn't know. You see, I'd been ill for quite some time . . ."

He silenced me with a gesture. "The penalty: you are forbidden to wear shoes for three days. Take off your shoes!"

I took off my shoes.

"Good God, man!" The official was struck with horror. "Leather shoes! Where did you get them? Are you completely out of your mind?"

"I may not be quite normal mentally, I myself can't judge. I bought the shoes a few years ago."

"Don't you know that the wearing of leather shoes in any shape or form by civilians is prohibited? —Your shoes are confiscated. And now let's see your identification papers!"

Merciful heavens, I had none!

"Incredible!" the official moaned. "Haven't seen anything like it in over a year!" He called in a policeman. "Take this man to Office 19, Room 8!"

I was driven barefoot through several streets. We went into another official building, passed through corridors, breathed the smell of paper and hopelessness; then I was pushed into a room and questioned by another official. This one was in uniform.

"You were picked up on the street without identification papers. You are fined two thousand gulden. I will make out your receipt immediately."

"I beg your pardon," I faltered. "I haven't that much money on me. Couldn't you lock me up for a while instead?"

He laughed aloud.

"Lock you up? My dear fellow, what an idea! Do you expect us to feed you in the bargain? —No, my friend, if you can't pay the trifling fine, I shall have to impose our heaviest penalty, temporary withdrawal of your existence permit! Kindly hand me your existence card!"

I had none.

The official was speechless. He called in two associates; they conferred in whispers, repeatedly motioning in my direction and looking at me with horror and amazement. Then my official had me led away to a detention room, pending deliberations on my case.

There several persons were sitting or standing about; a soldier stood guard at the door. I noticed that apart from my lack of shoes I was by far the best-dressed of the lot. The others treated me with a certain respect and made a seat free for me. A timid little man sidled up to me, bent down, and whispered in my ear: "I've got a magnificent bargain for you. I have a sugar beet at home. A whole sugar beet in perfect condition. It weighs almost seven pounds. Yours for the asking. What do you offer?"

He moved his ear close to my mouth, and I whispered: "You make me an offer. How much do you want?"

He whispered softly back: "Let's say a hundred and fifty gulden!"

I shook my head and looked away. Soon I was deep in thought.

I saw that I had been absent too long, it would be hard for me to adapt. I'd have given a good deal for a pair of shoes or stockings, my bare feet were miserably cold from the wet street. But everyone else in the room was barefoot too.

After a few hours they came for me. I was taken to Office 285, Room 19 f. This time the policeman stayed with me. He stationed himself between me and the official, a very high official, it seemed to me.

"You've put yourself in a very nasty position," he began. "You have been living in this city without an existence permit. You are aware no doubt that the heaviest penalties are in order."

I made a slight bow.

"If you please," I said, "I have only one request. I realize that I am quite unequal to the situation and that my position can only get worse and worse. —Couldn't you condemn me to death? I should be very grateful!"

The official looked gently into my eyes.

"I understand," he said amiably. "But anybody could come asking for that! In any case, you'd need a demise card. Can you afford one? They cost four thousand gulden."

"No, I haven't got that much money. But I'd give all I have. I have an enormous desire to die."

He smiled strangely.

"I can believe that, you're not the only one. But dying isn't so simple. You belong to the state, my dear man, you are obligated to the state, body and soul. You must know that. But by the way—I see you're registered under the name of Sinclair, Emil. Could you be Sinclair, the writer?"

"That's me!"

(25

"Oh, I'm so glad. Maybe I can do something for you. Officer, you may leave."

The policeman left the room, the official shook my hand.

"I've read your books with great interest," he said in a friendly tone, "and I'll do my best to help you. —But, good God, how did you get into this incredible situation?"

"Well, you see, I was away for a while. Two or three years ago I took refuge in the cosmic, and frankly I had rather supposed the war would be over by the time I got back. —But tell me, can you get me a demise card? I'd be ever so grateful."

"It may be possible. But first you'll need an existence permit. Obviously nothing can be done without that. I'll give you a note to Office 127. On my recommendation they'll issue you a temporary existence card. But it will only be valid for two days."

"Oh, that will be more than enough!"

"Very well! When you have it, come back here to me."

We shook hands.

"One more thing," I said softly. "May I ask you a question? You must realize how little I know about what's been going on."

"Go right ahead."

"Well, here's what I'd like to know: how can life go on under these conditions? How can people stand it?"

"Oh, they're not so badly off. Your situation is exceptional: a civilian—and without papers! There are very few civilians left. Practically everyone who isn't a soldier is a civil servant. That makes life bearable for most people, a good many are genuinely happy. Little by little one gets used to the shortages. When the potatoes gave out, we had to put up with sawdust gruel—they season it with tar now, it's surprisingly tasty—we all thought it would be unbearable. But then we got used to it. And the same with everything else."

"I see," I said. "It's really not so surprising. But there's one thing I still don't understand. Tell me: why is the whole world making these enormous efforts? Putting up with such hardships, with all these laws, these thousands of bureaus and bureaucrats—what is all this meant to preserve and safeguard?"

The gentleman looked at me in amazement.

"What a question!" he cried, shaking his head. "You know we're at war: the whole world is at war. That's what we are preserving, what we make laws and endure hardships for. The war! Without these enormous exertions and achievements our armies wouldn't be able to fight for a week. They'd starve—we can't allow that!"

"Yes," I said slowly, "you've got something there! The war, in other words, is a treasure that must be preserved at any cost. Yes, but—I know it's an odd question—why do you value the war so highly? Is it worth so much? Is war really a treasure?"

The official shrugged his shoulders and gave me a pitying look. He saw that I just didn't understand.

"My dear Herr Sinclair," he said. "You've lost contact with the world. Go out into the street, talk to people; then make a slight mental effort and ask yourself: What have we got left? What is the substance of our lives? Only one answer is possible: The war is all we have left! Pleasure and personal profit, social ambition, greed, love, cultural

(27

activity—all that has gone out of existence. If there is still any law, order, or thought in the world, we have the war to thank for it. —Now do you understand?"

Yes, now I understood, and I thanked the gentleman kindly.

I left him and mechanically pocketed the recommendation to Office 127. I had no intention of using it, I had no desire to molest the gentlemen in those offices any further. Before anyone could notice me and stop me, I inwardly recited the short astral spell, turned off my heartbeat, and made my body vanish under a clump of bushes. I pursued my cosmic wanderings and abandoned the idea of going home.

Christmas
December 1917

Even before the Great Reminder, I always felt
vague misgivings at Christmas time, an unpleasant taste in my mouth. Here was something pretty but
not quite authentic, something universally trusted and respected but which nevertheless inspired a certain secret
distrust.

Now that the fourth wartime Christmas is coming, I
cannot dispel that taste in my mouth. True, I shall celebrate Christmas, because I have children and wouldn't
want to deprive them of a pleasure. But I shall celebrate
this children's Christmas in the same spirit as I celebrate
the prisoners' Christmas in the course of my war work—
as an official gesture, a concession to a time-worn tradition, a dusty sentimentality. For the past three years we
have been treating these unfortunate prisoners of war like
hardened criminals, and now we send them pretty little
boxes and packages with snippets of evergreen in them—
it's touching, sometimes I myself am moved, I imagine
the feelings of a prisoner who receives his little present,
the flood of memories that come over him as he smells his
bit of evergreen. But at bottom that too is sentimentality.

All year long we keep the prisoners in confinement,
though they have done nothing but let themselves be
surprised by enemy action, and then on Christmas we

visit these unfortunate hundreds of thousands or millions with tender gifts and remind them of the feast of love. That is just how we treat our children. Once a year we invite them to rejoice in the legend of divine love; for one evening, under the Christmas tree, we are touchingly attentive to them, while all the rest of the time we bring them up to shoulder the very fate that we all curse.

When a prisoner of war throws the pretty Christmas package I have sent him in my face and tramples the sentimental evergreen, he is perfectly right. And when our children are not quite able to believe in our emotion, our beatitude in the presence of the Christ child, when they regard us as a wee bit hypocritical or ridiculous, they too are perfectly right. Except for a few sincerely religious people, our Christmas has long been sheer sentimentality. Or worse: a basis for advertising campaigns, a field for dishonest enterprise, for the manufacture of kitsch.

Why? Because for all of us, Christmas, the feast of childlike love, has long ceased to be the expression of a genuine feeling. It has become the exact opposite, a substitute for feeling, a cheap imitation. Once a year we behave as though we attached great importance to noble sentiments, as though it rejoiced us to spend money on them. Actually, our passing emotion at the real beauty of such feelings may be very great; the greater and more genuine it is, the greater the sentimentality. Sentimentality is our typical attitude toward Christmas and the few other outward occasions on which vestiges of the Christian order still enter into our lives. Our feeling on such occasions is this: "This idea of love is a great thing!" How true that only love can redeem us! And what a pity that our circumstances allow us the luxury of this noble sentiment only once a year, that our business and other important concerns keep us away from it all the rest of the time! Such feeling has all the earmarks of sentimentality. Because it is sentimentality to comfort ourselves with feelings that we do not take seriously enough to make sacrifices for, to convert into actions.

When the priests and the pious complain that faith has vanished from the world and happiness with it, they are right. Our attitude toward all true human values is more barbarous and insensitive than anything the world has seen for centuries. This is evident in our attitude toward religion, in our attitude toward art, and in our art itself. For the widespread opinion that modern Europe has risen to unprecedented heights in art, or in "culture" for that matter, is the invention of our culture-philistines.

The "cultivated" man of today takes a characteristic attitude toward the teachings of Jesus: all year long he neither gives them a thought nor lives by them, but on Christmas Eve he gives way to a vague, melancholy childhood memory and wallows in cheap, tame, pious sentiments, just as once or twice a year, while listening to the St. Matthew Passion for instance, he makes his bow to this long-forgotten but still troubling and secretly powerful world.

Everyone admits as much, everyone knows it, and everyone also knows that it's very sad. We are told that political and economic developments are to blame, or the state, or militarism, and so on. Because something must be to blame. No nation "wanted the war," just as no nation wanted the fourteen-hour day, the housing shortage, or the high rate of infant mortality.

Before we celebrate another Christmas, before we try once again to appease our one eternal and truly important yearning with mass-produced imitation sentiment, let us face up to our wretched situation. No idea or principle is to blame for all our wretchedness, for the nullity, the coarseness, the barrenness of our lives, for war and hunger and everything else that is evil and dismal; we ourselves are to blame. And it is only through ourselves, through our insight and our will, that a change can come about.

It makes no difference whether we go back to the teachings of Jesus and make them our own again, or whether we seek new forms. Where they strike the eternal core of humanity, the teachings of Jesus and of Lao-tzu, of the Vedas and of Goethe are the same. There is only one doctrine. There is only one religion. There is only one happiness. There are a thousand forms, a thousand heralds, but only one call, one voice. The voice of God does not come from Mount Sinai, it does not come from the Bible. The essence of love, beauty, and holiness does not reside in Christianity or in antiquity or in Goethe or Tolstoy—it resides in you, in you and me, in each one of us. This is the one eternal and forever identical doctrine, our one eternal truth. It is the doctrine of the "Kingdom of Heaven" that we bear within ourselves.

Light the Christmas candles for your children! Let them sing carols! But don't delude yourselves, don't content yourselves year after year with the shabby, pathetic, sentimental feeling you have when you celebrate your holidays! Demand more of yourselves! Love and joy and the mysterious thing we call "happiness" are not over here or over there, they are only "within ourselves."

Shall There Be Peace?
December 1917

O NLY RECENTLY Wilson and Lloyd George proclaimed their unswerving will to fight on till final
victory. In the Italian Chamber the Socialist Mergari was
treated like a madman because he had spoken a few natural, human words. And today, with what wooden self-
righteousness a Wolff dispatch denies the rumor of a new
German peace proposal: "Germany and its allies have not
the slightest reason for repeating their magnanimous offer
of peace."

In other words, everything goes on as before, and if
anywhere a peaceful blade of grass tries to pierce the
ground, a military boot is quick to trample it.

Yet at the same time we read that peace negotiations
have begun in Brest-Litovsk, that Herr Kühlmann has
opened the session with a reference to the significance of
Christmas and has spoken, in the words of the Gospel, of
peace on earth. If he means what he says, if he has even
the faintest understanding of those tremendous words,
peace is inevitable. Unfortunately, our experience of
Bible quotations in the mouths of statesmen has not thus
far been encouraging.

For many days now the eyes of the world have been
focused upon two places. In those two places, it is widely
felt, the destinies of nations are coming to a head, the

future beckoning, and disaster threatening. With bated breath the world is looking eastward, to the peace negotiations in Brest-Litovsk. And at the same time it is watching the western front in dire anguish, for everyone feels, everyone knows that, short of a miracle, the most dreadful disaster that has ever befallen men is there impending: the bitterest, bloodiest, most ruthless and appalling battle of all time.

Everyone knows it and everyone, with the exception of a few sanguine political orators and war profiteers, is trembling at the thought. Concerning the outcome of this mass slaughter, opinions and hopes vary. In both camps there is a minority who seriously believe in a decisive victory. But one thing that no one endowed with a vestige of good sense can believe is that the ideal, humanitarian aims, which figure so prominently in the speeches of all our statesmen, will be achieved. The bigger, the bloodier, the more destructive these final battles of the World War prove to be, the less will be accomplished for the future, the less hope there will be of appeasing hatreds and rivalries, or of doing away with the idea that political aims can be attained by the criminal instrumentality of war. If one camp should indeed achieve final victory (and this purpose is the one justification offered by the leaders in their incendiary speeches), then what we abhor as "militarism" will have won out. If in their secret heart the partisans of war mean so much as a single word of what they have been saying about war aims, the absurdity, the utter futility of all their arguments staggers the imagination.

Can a new massacre of inconceivable scope be justified by such a jumble of hopeless fallacies, of mutually con-

tradictory hopes and plans? While all peoples with even
the slightest experience of war and its suffering are await-
ing the outcome of the Russian peace negotiations in
prayer and expectation, while all of us are moved to love
and gratitude for the Russians because they, first among
nations, have attacked the war at its root and resolved to
end it, while half the world is going hungry and useful
human effort has been halved where it has not ceased
altogether—at such a time, preparations are being made
in France for what we shudder even to name, a mass
slaughter which is expected to decide, but will not decide, the outcome of the war, for the final senseless
mustering of heroism and patience, the final hideous tri-
umph of dynamite and machines over human life and the
human spirit!

In view of this situation it is our duty, the one sacred
duty of every man of good will on earth, not to sheathe
ourselves in indifference and let things take their course,
but to do our utmost to prevent this final catastrophe.

Yes, you say, but what can we do? If we were statesmen and ministers, we would do our bit, but, as it is, we
have no power!

This is the easy reaction to all responsibility—until it
becomes too pressing. If we turn to the politicians and
leaders, they too shake their heads and invoke their help-
lessness. We cannot sit back and put the blame on
them.

To blame are the inertia and cowardice of each one of
us, our obstinacy and reluctance to think. In response to
the excellent Mergari, Sonnino refused to say "anything
that might give aid and comfort to the enemy"; the Wolff
dispatch I have just mentioned declares that Germany

has "not the slightest reason" to make another move in behalf of peace. But every day we ourselves give evidence of the same attitude. We accept things as they come, we rejoice in victories, we deplore the losses in our own camp, we tacitly accept war as an instrument of politics.

Alas, every nation and every family, every single individual in all Europe and far beyond it, has more than enough "reason" to give his utmost in behalf of the peace for which we all yearn. Only a vanishing minority of men truly want the war to go on—and beyond a doubt they deserve our contempt and sincerest hatred. No one else, only a very few morbid fanatics or unscrupulous criminals are in favor of this war, and yet—inconceivable as it seems—it goes on and on, with both sides arming indefatigably for the allegedly final holocaust in the West!

This is possible only because we are all too lazy, too easygoing, too cowardly. It is possible only because somewhere in our secret hearts we approve or tolerate the war, because we throw all the resources of our minds and souls to the winds and let the misguided machines roll on! That is what the political leaders do, and what the armies do, but we ourselves, the onlookers, are no better. We all know that we can stop the war if we want to in earnest. We know that whenever men have felt an action to be truly necessary they have performed it against all resistance. We have looked on with admiration and beating hearts as the Russians laid down their arms and manifested their will to make peace. There is no people on earth that has not been profoundly moved in its heart and conscience by this marvelous drama. But at the same moment we reject the obligations such feelings imply.

Every politician in the world is all in favor of revolution, reason, and the laying down of arms—but only in the enemy camp, not in his own! If we are in earnest, we can stop the war. Once again the Russians have exemplified the ancient and holy doctrine that the weak can be mightiest. Why does no one follow them? Why do parliaments and cabinets everywhere content themselves with the same dreary drivel, the same day-to-day trivialities, why do they nowhere rise up to champion a great idea, the only idea that matters today? Why do they favor the self-determination of nations only when they themselves hope to profit? Why are people still taken in by the false idealism of official phrasemongers? It has been said that every nation has the rulers it wants and deserves. Maybe so. We Europeans at all events have the bloodiest and most ruthless of all rulers: war. Is that what we want and deserve?

No, we don't want it. We all want the opposite. Apart from a small number of profiteers, no one wants this shameful and dismal state of affairs. What then can we do? We can bestir ourselves! We can take every opportunity to manifest our readiness for peace. We can desist from such useless provocations as the above-mentioned Wolff dispatch, and stop talking like Sonnino. At the present juncture a slight humiliation, a concession, a humane impulse can do us no harm! How, when we have befouled ourselves so thoroughly with blood, can we worry about petty national vanities?

Now is the time to oust those statesmen who conceive foreign policy in terms of self-seeking national programs, who ignore the cry of mankind! Why wait until their stupidity has shed the blood of more millions?

All of us—great and small, belligerents and neutrals—
we must not close our ears to the dire warning of this
hour, the threat of such unthinkable horrors. Peace is at
hand! As a thought, a desire, a suggestion, as a power
working in silence, it is everywhere, in every heart. If
each one of us opens his heart to it, if each one of us
firmly resolves to serve the cause of peace, to communi-
cate his thoughts and intimations of peace—if every man
of good will decides to devote himself exclusively for a
little while to clearing away the obstacles, the barriers to
peace, then we shall have peace.

If that is done we shall all have helped to bring it
about, we shall all feel worthy of the great tasks it will
impose—whereas hitherto we have all been possessed by
a feeling of shared guilt.

If the War Goes on
Another Five Years
Early in 1918

In the autumn of 1925, the Official Journal, *the one newspaper still published (weekly) in the Kingdom of Saxony, carried the following short article with the somewhat recondite headline:*

A NEW KASPAR HAUSER

NEAR RONNEBURG in Vogtland a puzzling and troubling discovery was recently made. Only the future can show whether it should be regarded as a mere curiosity or as a matter of more far-reaching interest.

In the course of the "elimination of citizens demonstrably unfit for public service," a program which in our district has been organized with exemplary efficiency and, allowing for inevitable hardships, humanely executed, the Ronneburg regional authorities have reported one of those all-too-frequent cases in which a private individual, despite his demonstrated inability to be of any further use whatsoever to the state and common weal, appreciably oversteps his allotted existence time, in the present instance by several months, it appears. A year before, the old-age control board had classified this private individual, one Philipp Gassner residing in a secluded country house outside one of the villages, as unemployable and, as usual in such cases, reminded him of his civic duty by progressive reduction of his rations. When his deadline expired, his demise had not been reported, nor had an appointment been made in his name with the regional chloroform center. Thereupon the regional authorities sent Sergeant Kille to Gassner's place of residence to convey a formal notification of his civic duty and inform him of the penalty for noncompliance.

Although this notification was communicated in the accepted forms and accompanied by the usual offer of free service, Gassner, a man of almost seventy, was thrown into a state of extraordinary agitation and obstinately refused to comply with the law. In vain the sergeant rebuked him for his unpatriotic attitude and tried to make him see how disheartening it was that an old man, grown gray in civic honors, should decline to make the sacrifice which all our hopeful young men were prepared to make at the front. When the sergeant pronounced him under arrest, Gassner went so far as to resist. The sergeant, who had already been struck by the physical strength of this man who had been put on diminishing rations, proceeded to search the house. And now comes the incredible part of the story: a young male was discovered in a second-floor room overlooking the garden. The old man had been hiding him for years!

This young man, aged twenty-six and brimming with health, turned out to be Alois Gassner, the house owner's son. How the sly old man was able to elude the conscription authority and keep his son hidden for years remains to be clarified; the most likely hypothesis would seem to be a criminal falsification of the records. Much is explained, no doubt, by the secluded location of the house, by the father's ample means, and by the existence of a carefully cultivated kitchen garden which provided them both with more than sufficient food.

What interests us here is not so much the unusual case of grave fraud and draft evasion, as a psychological anomaly which has come to light and is now being investigated by experts. The story is hardly believable, but the testimony at hand leaves no room for doubt!

The specialists all agree that Alois Gassner is mentally normal. In addition to his skill in reading, writing, and arithmetic, he is highly cultivated and, with the help of a well-stocked private library, has devoted himself to the study of philosophy. He has written a number of papers on epistemology and various aspects of the history of philosophy, not to mention poems and excursions in creative writing, all of which bear witness at the very least to clear thinking and a trained mind.

But there is a most unusual gap in this strange young man's mental life—he knows nothing of the war! All these years he has lived outside of the world that surrounds us all! Just as officially he did not exist for the world, so our world and our times did not exist for him. He is probably the only adult in Europe who, though of perfectly sound mind, knows nothing whatever of his times, of the World War, of the events and upheavals of the last ten years!

We are tempted to compare this strange philosopher with Kaspar Hauser, that legendary figure whose early years were spent in a secluded twilight, removed from the world of men.

It will probably not take long to elucidate and pass judgment on the relatively simple case of Gassner Senior. He has committed a grave offense and will have to take the consequences. But, as to the guilt or complicity of the son, opinions vary widely. At present he is still under examination in a mental hospital. His only reaction to what little he has thus far learned about current events, the state, and his civic duties, has been childlike wonder tinged with fear. It is quite evident that he does not take the attempts to educate him in these matters very seriously; he seems to regard all references to the present-day world as fictions employed to test his mental condition. So far, questions and association tests based on common catchwords familiar to every child have elicited no response.

We learn, on the point of going to press, that the philosophical faculty of Leipzig University is now looking into the case. Gassner's writings are to be examined. But, regardless of the positive or negative value of these writings, the faculty is most eager to make the acquaintance of the man himself and may decide to acquire him as the sole exemplar of an otherwise extinct species of man. This "prewar man" will be subjected to thorough investigation and perhaps preserved for science.

The European
January 1918

A<small>T LAST</small> the Lord God relented and sent the great flood, so putting an end to the era in the history of the earth that had culminated in the bloody World War. Compassionately the waters washed away what had desecrated the aging planet, the blood-drenched snow fields and the mountains bristling with cannon, the rotting corpses along with those who mourned them, those drunk with blood lust along with the impoverished, the starving along with those who had gone mad.

Mildly the blue sky looked down on the smooth ball.

To the very end European technology had shown its mettle. For weeks Europe had defended itself ably and stubbornly against the slowly rising waters. At first with enormous dikes on which millions of war prisoners worked day and night; then with artificial mounds that rose up with fabulous speed and at first looked like gigantic terraces but gradually tapered into towers. Withdrawing to these towers, men kept faith to the last with the touching heroism of their kind. First Europe, then the whole world had been submerged, but on the last emerging towers searchlights still darted their glaring beams into the moist twilight, while cannon lobbed their projectiles from tower to tower in graceful arcs. The heroic shell fire was maintained to the end.

At length the whole world was flooded. Sustained by a life belt, the sole surviving European drifted about in the waters, employing his last strength to record the events of the last days, for he wished the men of the future to know that *his* fatherland had outlived its enemies by several hours, so securing the palm of victory for all time.

Then an enormous black hulk appeared on the gray horizon and slowly approached the exhausted European. To his delight, he recognized the ark, he saw the aged patriarch standing on the deck—an imposing figure with a flowing gray beard—and then he lost consciousness. A gigantic African fished him out of the water. Soon he opened his eyes and there stood the patriarch smiling, for now the success of his mission was complete: a specimen of every variety of living creature on earth had been saved.

While the ark ran leisurely before the wind, waiting for the muddy waters to recede, a merry life took shape. Great schools of fish followed in the vessel's wake, birds and insects of every color swarmed over the open deck, every animal and every human being was filled with rejoicing at having been saved and reserved for a new life. The pied peacock sent its shrill morning cry out over the waters, the elephant laughed and showered himself and his wife out of his upraised trunk, the lizard lay iridescent on a sun-drenched timber. With swift thrusts of his harpoon the Indian gathered glittering fishes out of the infinite flood waters; the African made fire by rubbing dry sticks together and in his joy beat a rhythmic tattoo on his plump wife's thighs with the flat of his hand. The Hindu stood thin and straight with folded arms, muttering verses of ancient songs of Creation. The Eskimo lay steaming in the sun, sweating water and blubber, and his little eyes laughed as a good-natured tapir sniffed at him. The little Japanese had cut himself a wand, which he held carefully balanced, sometimes on his nose, sometimes on his chin. The European, whose writing materials had been saved with him, drew up an inventory of the living creatures present.

Groups and friendships formed, and whenever a quarrel seemed to be starting up, the patriarch quickly stopped it with a wave of his hand. All were sociable and merry, only the European held aloof, busy with his writing. —And then all the many-colored humans and animals devised a game, a contest in which each one would display his skills. Everyone wanted to be first, and the patriarch himself had to keep order. He divided his passengers into separate groups: large animals, small animals, and humans. First everyone had to speak up and announce the feat in which he expected to excel, and then each performed in turn.

This fine game went on for many days, because the members of each group would suddenly stop what they were doing and run off to watch another group. What wonderful things there were to be seen! Each of God's creatures showed its hidden talents. What a splendid display of life's riches! And how they laughed, how they sang, crowed, clapped, stamped, and neighed their applause!

The weasel ran brilliantly, the lark sang enchantingly, the proud-chested turkey-cock marched magnificently, and the squirrel climbed with incredible dexterity. The mandrill imitated the Malay and the baboon imitated the mandrill. Runners and climbers, swimmers and fliers contested untiringly, and each in his way was unexcelled and applauded as such. Certain animals wrought magic and others made themselves invisible. Many distinguished themselves by strength, others by guile, some in the attack, others in the defensive. Insects showed how they could protect themselves by making themselves look like grass, wood, moss, or rock, while others among the weak won applause and put the laughing onlookers to flight by emitting dreadful smells to ward off attack. No one held back, all had their talents. Birds' nests were plaited, pasted, woven, and cemented. Birds of prey showed how they could recognize the tiniest thing from dizzy heights.

The humans also performed well. Nimbly and without effort the big African clambered up the mast; with three deft movements the Malay transformed a palm leaf into a paddle and rode out over the waters on a small plank. The Indian hit the smallest target with a light arrow, and from two kinds of bast his wife plaited a mat that won loud admiration. All were struck dumb with amazement at the Hindu's feats of magic. And the Chinese showed how an industrious people trebled the wheat harvest by digging up the seedlings and transplanting them at regular intervals.

The European was very unpopular. Several times he had aroused the hostility of his human cousins by belittling the accomplishments of others. When the Indian shot a bird high up in the sky, the white man shrugged his shoulders and declared that he could shoot three times as high with an ounce of dynamite. When challenged to do it, he had hemmed and hawed and said he would need this and that and a dozen other things. He had also ridiculed the Chinese, saying yes, this transplanting of wheat seedlings did show that his people were industrious, but he doubted whether such back-breaking toil could make them happy. The Chinese had won general approval by replying that any people which had enough to eat and honored the gods was happy, but at that too the European had scoffed.

The merry contest went on, and at length all the animals and all the humans had displayed their talents and skills. All were impressed and pleased with one another. The patriarch had laughed into his white beard and said in token of praise that now the waters could cheerfully subside, for a new and infinitely happy life was in the offing.

Only the European performed no feat, and now they all clamored that he should step forward and do his bit, to show whether he too had a right to breathe God's good air and ride in the patriarch's floating house. For a long while he refused and made excuses. But then Noah himself intervened. Whereupon the white man spoke up. "I too," he said, "have developed an ability and trained it to high proficiency. My eye is no keener than that of other beings, nor does my distinction reside in my ear or nose or in any manual skill or in anything of the kind. My gift is of a higher nature. My gift is the intellect."

"Show us!" cried the African, and all pressed close.

"It cannot be shown," said the white man gently. "Perhaps you have not understood me. What distinguishes me is my mind."

The African laughed gaily, showing his snow-white teeth; the Hindu curled his thin lips in mockery; the Chinese smiled a shrewd, good-natured smile.

"Intellect?" he said slowly. "Do please show us this intellect of yours. So far we haven't seen a thing."

"There's nothing to see," said the European sulkily.

"My special gift is this: in my head I store up images of the outside world. From these images, I make for myself new images and systems. I am able to think the whole world in my brain; in other words, to make it over."

Noah passed his hand over his eyes.

"I beg your pardon," he said slowly, "but what is the good of that? God has already created the world once. Why would you want to create it again and keep it in your little head all for yourself?"

Cries of applause and eager questions shot from all sides.

"Hold on," said the European. "You don't understand. The work of the intellect cannot be demonstrated like some other art or craft."

The Hindu smiled. "Oh yes it can, white cousin, oh yes it can. Show us the work of your intellect. Reckoning, for instance. Let's have a reckoning contest. Here now: a man and his wife have three children, each of whom in turn founds a family. Each of the young couples has a child each year. How many years will it be before we have a hundred people in all?"

All listened eagerly, knitted their brows and counted on their fingers. The European tried hard. But he had scarcely begun to reckon when the Chinese announced the answer. "Not bad," the white man admitted, "but that's just mental agility. My intellect isn't meant for little tricks, it's meant for great problems on which the happiness of mankind depends."

"Splendid," said Noah encouragingly. "The skill that brings happiness is certainly more important than any other. Just tell us what you know about the happiness of mankind. We shall all be grateful." The assembly waited spellbound for the white man to speak. Now we shall know! Honor be to him who will show us where the happiness of man is to be found! We beg his forgiveness for all our unkind words! If he knows that, what need has he of the skills of eye, ear, or hand, of persevering toil or arithmetic!

Up until then the European had been haughty and self-assured. Now, in the face of their respectful curiosity, he seemed at a loss.

"It's not my fault," he said hesitantly, "but you still don't understand. I didn't say I knew the secret of happiness. I only said that my intellect is working on certain problems the solution of which would promote the happiness of mankind. Such work takes a long time, neither you nor I will live to see the end of it. The problems are knotty and many generations will continue to ponder them."

The audience listened with mounting perplexity and distrust. What was the man saying? Even Noah averted his eyes and frowned.

The Hindu smiled at the Chinese. When the others could think of nothing to say, the Chinese spoke up. "Dear brothers," he said most affably, "this white cousin is a joker. He is trying to tell us that his mind is working on something which our great-grandchildren's great-grandchildren may or may not live to see. I suggest that we applaud him as a joker. He says things that none of us can quite understand, but we all suspect that if we did fully understand them they would make us laugh and laugh and laugh. Don't you all feel the same way? —Glad to hear it. I propose three cheers for our joker!"

Most of the humans and animals joined in and were

glad the distressing incident was over. But some were disgruntled and angry, and the European was left very much to himself. Late in the afternoon the African, accompanied by the Eskimo, the Indian, and the Malay, went to the patriarch and said:

"Revered father, we have a question to ask you. We don't like that white fellow who made fun of us. Every single animal, every bear and every flea, every pheasant and every dung beetle, and each of us humans as well, has had something to show, some talent with which we honor God and protect, enhance, or beautify our lives. We have seen astonishing gifts, and some have made us laugh; but even the smallest creature had something gratifying to offer—only that pale fellow we fished up last offered nothing but strange, arrogant words, nothing but allusions and jokes that no one understood and that gave no one any pleasure. —And so, dear father, we ask you: is it fitting that such a creature should join in starting a new life on this beloved earth? Mightn't the results be disastrous? Just look at him! His eyes are cloudy, his brow is full of wrinkles, his hands are pale and feeble, his face is sullen and sad, altogether he radiates gloom. There must be something wrong with him—God knows who sent the fellow to our ark!"

The aged patriarch raised his friendly eyes to his questioners.

"My children," he said slowly and so kindly that their faces brightened, "my dear children! What you say is both right and wrong. But God had already given his answer before you asked me your question. I can't help agreeing that the man from the war country is not very prepossessing, and it's hard to see why such cranks should exist. But God, who created his species, must know why. All of you have ample grievances against the white men, they were the ones who corrupted our poor earth and brought this judgment upon it. But behold, God has given us a sign of what he had in mind in saving this white man. All of you, you the African, you the Indian, and you the Eskimo, have your beloved wives with you for the new life that we hope to begin soon on earth. Only the man from Europe is alone. For a long time that dismayed me, but now I think I know the reason. This man has been preserved as a warning and a goad to us, perhaps as a kind of ghost. But he will not be able to perpetuate himself, except by plunging back into the stream of multicolored mankind. He will not be able to corrupt your life on the new earth. Be assured of that!"

Night fell, and in the morning the pointed summit of the Holy Mountain emerged from the waters.

Dream after Work
March 1918

I N MY POST of deputy secretary in a government department, I find myself in pretty much the same situation as most of those who were obliged some years ago to relinquish their old habits and have been harnessed to the service ever since. For days on end the work keeps us in a state of tension, we go to bed with it and get up with it, we worry about our departments, we cast about for better, simpler methods, and plunge our whole personality into the crucible of the times. And then suddenly a moment comes when our own self—the "old Adam" of the theologians—stirs within us, lethargic and uncertain as a man trying to wake from anesthesia, who has not yet gained full control over his limbs or his thoughts.

That is how I felt the other day as I was strolling home from the office with a bundle of dossiers under my arm. The sun was warm, the air held a foretaste of spring and smelled as if the hazelnut bushes must somewhere be in flower. Only a moment before, in the streetcar, my thoughts had been busy with my prisoners of war, I had mulled over the letters and memoranda I was planning to write after dinner. Now I was on my way out of the city, and suddenly my thoughts were no longer with the prisoners, the censorship, the paper shortage, or the difficulty in obtaining credits. From one minute to the next I saw the world as it looks when we are free from care. Plump blackbirds darted through the bare hedges and the lime trees bordering the farms etched the fine network of their branches into the blue, lightly clouded spring sky. Here and there on the fringes of the fields there were patches of glistening fresh green, and the light played over the lush moss on the trunks of the walnut trees. Everything I was carrying in my briefcase and in my head was forgotten, and for a quarter of an hour, while my walk lasted, I lived not in what we call "reality" but in the beautiful authentic reality we bear within us. I did what children and lovers and poets do. I forgot all will and purpose and let myself drift in pursuit of lovely, colorful dreams.

Wishful dreams! They passed before my eyes and as I watched them I caught sight of things that struck me as new, conceived that day for the first time. I discerned a pure, innocent, unblemished egoism, a round, self-sufficient world of egoistic, amoral, asocial desires and images of the future. Nothing to do with war and peace, nothing to do with the exchange of prisoners, and nothing to do with the art, society, school system, or religion of the future. Such concerns did not reach into the depths, they were only on the surface. For once my old Adam stripped off the veils; he was a child and all his desires related to himself and his little well-being.

I had a wonderful dream. I dreamed that peace had come, we had all been discharged and gone off, the sun was shining and I could do exactly as I pleased.

I did three things in my dreams. First I lay on an ocean beach with my feet in the water. I gnawed at a blade of grass, my eyes were half closed, and I hummed a tune. From time to time I tried to recollect what the tune I was humming was, but it was too much trouble. What did I care? I went on humming until I had enough and splashed my feet in the water. I almost fell asleep in the warm sun, but suddenly it all came back to me: I was free and my own master, I could do whatever I liked, I was lying on a beach, and far and wide there was no one but me. I jumped up, let out an Indian war whoop, and threw myself with a splash into the blue water. I thrashed about, swam out and back, felt hungry, ran up on the beach, shook the water out of my hair, and lay down beside my open knapsack. Slowly I took out a thick slice of bread, excellent prewar black bread, and a sausage— the kind of sausage we took with us on school picnics as boys—a chunk of Swiss cheese and an apple and a piece of chocolate. I spread all these things out before me and looked at them until I could bear it no longer. Then I pounced on them. And as I chewed, a remote, forgotten childhood happiness flowed from the bread and sausage and engulfed me completely.

But not for long. Soon the scene changed. Now I was serious and fully dressed, sitting in a cool room overlooking a garden. The shadows of branches played over the windows. In my lap I held a book in which I was utterly immersed. I didn't know what the book was. I only knew that it was philosophy—but not Kant or Plato, more on the order of Angelus Silesius—and I read and read and steeped myself in the ineffable joy of plunging free and undisturbed, without yesterday or tomorrow, into this sea, this beautiful, inexhaustible sea of attention and exaltation, of eagerly anticipated events that would justify me and confirm my thinking. I read and mused, slowly I turned the pages, in the window a golden-brown bee sang and buzzed as though the whole silent world were inside it, desiring nothing more than to express its glutted quietness and contentment.

From time to time it seemed to me that from the distance, or from inside the house, I heard delicate noble sounds, a violin or a cello. Little by little they became louder and more real, and my reading and thinking became a hearing, a voluptuous immersion. The measures of Mozart governed an appeased, pure world.

And once again my dream changed. As though I had been there all my life, I was sitting on a camp chair beside a low wall at the edge of a vineyard in a southern valley. On my knees I had a small square of cardboard, in my left hand a light palette, and in my right hand a brush. Beside me my walking stick was planted in the soft ground, my knapsack lay open, and I could see the little pinched tubes of paint in it. I took one out, unscrewed the cap, and with profound joy squeezed a bit of the purest cobalt blue out onto my palette, and then some white and a fine Veronese green for the evening air, and the barest pinch of Turkey red. For a long time I peered at the distant mountains and the smoky golden-brown clouds, and mixed ultramarine into the red, holding my breath in caution because the scene had to be so infinitely delicate and light and airy. After a moment's hesitation my brush, with swift circular strokes, painted a luminous cloud into the blue, with gray and violet shadows. The barely intimated greens of the foreground and of the leafy chestnut trees began to play upon one another and enter into a harmony with the muffled red and blue of the background. The friendships and affections of the colors, their attractions and enmities rang out, and soon all the life within me was concentrated in the little square of card-board on my knees. Everything the world had to say and do to me, to confess to me and ask my forgiveness for—and I to the world—lay there ardent and still in the white and blue, in the bold joyful yellow and the sweet serene green. And I felt that this was life! This was my share in the world, my joy and my burden. Here I was at home. Here there was pleasure in store for me, here I was king, here I could turn my back with blissful indifference on the whole official world.

A shadow fell on my little picture, I looked up—I was standing outside my house and the dream was over.

War and Peace
Summer 1918

U NDOUBTEDLY those who call war the primordial
and natural state are right. Insofar as man is an
animal, he lives by struggle, he lives at the expense of
others, whom he fears and hates. Life then is war.

"Peace" is much harder to define. Peace is neither an
original paradisiacal state nor a form of coexistence by
mutual consent. Peace is something we do not know; we
can only sense it and search for it. Peace is an ideal. It is
infinitely complex, unstable and fragile—a breath can destroy it. True peace is more difficult and unusual than any
other ethical or intellectual achievement—even for two
persons who live together and need each other.

And yet the ideal of peace, the desire for peace are age-
old. For thousands of years we have known the mighty
and fundamental maxim: "Thou shalt not kill." More than
by any other trait, man is characterized by his capacity
for such maxims, such far-reaching imperatives; it distinguishes him from the animals and seems to draw a line
between him and "nature."

Man, we feel in the presence of such mighty maxims, is
not an animal; he is not a determinate, finite entity, not a
being completed once and for all, but a coming-into-
being, a project, a dream of the future, a yearning of
nature for new forms and possibilities. When first uttered,

(57

the commandment "Thou shalt not kill" was enormous in scope. It was almost synonymous with "Thou shalt not breathe"! It was seemingly impossible, insane, and self-destructive. And yet this maxim has retained its power down through the ages, it has created laws, attitudes, and ethical doctrines; few other maxims have borne such fruit and so revolutionized the life of man.

"Thou shalt not kill" is not a cut-and-dried formula of schoolroom "altruism." Altruism does not occur in nature. "Thou shalt not kill" does not mean: don't harm the other man! It means: don't deprive yourself of the other man, don't harm yourself! The other man is not a stranger; he is not something remote, unrelated to me, and self-sufficient. Everything in the world, all the thousands of "others," exist for me only insofar as I see them, feel them, have relations with them. Relations between me and the world, between me and "others," are the substance of my life.

To know this, to sense it and grope one's way toward this complex truth, has been the path of mankind. There has been progress and regression. Luminous ideas have flared up, out of which we proceeded to build dark laws, caverns of conscience. There have been strange developments such as gnosis and alchemy, which, though some of our contemporaries put them down as absurdities, may well have been high points in man's search for insight. And out of alchemy, which began as a path to the purest mysticism and the ultimate fulfillment of the "Thou shalt not kill," we have, with smiling arrogance, created a science and technology that manufacture explosives and poison gases. Where is the progress? Where the regression? There is neither.

The great war of these last years also has shown both faces. It appears to have brought both progress and regression. Its cruel techniques of mass murder have suggested regression, seeming indeed to mock the whole idea of progress or of culture. Yet certain new needs, insights, and strivings engendered by the war have struck us as a kind of progress. One journalist has felt justified in disposing of inward stirrings as "introverted rubbish"—but may he not have been very much mistaken? Is it not quite conceivable that his crude gibe was directed toward what is best, most essential, and most vital in our times?

Be that as it may, one opinion that has often been expressed in the course of the war is absolutely mistaken: the opinion that, through its sheer magnitude and the gigantic mechanism of horror it set in motion, this war would frighten future generations out of ever making war again. Fear teaches men nothing. If men enjoy killing, no memory of war will deter them. Nor will the knowledge of the material damage wrought by war. Only in infinitesimal degree do men's actions spring from rational considerations. One can be thoroughly convinced that an action is absurd and still delight in it. Every passionate man does just that.

That is why I am not, as many of my friends and enemies suppose, a pacifist. I no more believe that world peace can be brought about in rational ways, by preaching, organization, and propaganda, than that the philosopher's stone can be invented by a congress of chemists.

What then can give rise to a true spirit of peace on earth? Not commandments and not practical experience. Like all human progress, the love of peace must come from knowledge. All living knowledge as opposed to aca-

(59

demic knowledge can have but one object. This knowledge may be seen and formulated by thousands in a thousand different ways, but it must always embody one truth. It is the knowledge of the living substance in us, in each of us, in you and me, of the secret magic, the secret godliness that each of us bears within him. It is the knowledge that, starting from this innermost point, we can at all times transcend all pairs of opposites, transforming white into black, evil into good, night into day. The Indians call it "Atman," the Chinese "Tao"; Christians call it "grace." Where that supreme knowledge is present (as in Jesus, Buddha, Plato, or Lao-tzu), a threshold is crossed beyond which miracles begin. There war and enmity cease. We can read of it in the New Testament and in the discourses of Gautama. Anyone who is so inclined can laugh at it and call it "introverted rubbish," but to one who has experienced it his enemy becomes a brother, death becomes birth, disgrace honor, calamity good fortune. Each thing on earth discloses itself twofold, as "of this world" and "not of this world." But "this world" means what is "outside us." Everything that is outside us can become enemy, danger, fear and death. The light dawns with the experience that this entire "outward" world is not only an object of our perception but at the same time the creation of our soul, with the transformation of all outward into inward things, of the world into the self.

What I am saying is self-evident. But just as every soldier shot to death is the eternal repetition of an error, so the truth must be repeated forever and ever in a thousand forms.

History
November 1918

WHEN I WAS A BOY attending a bad Latin school, what was known as "history" seemed to me as infinitely venerable, remote, noble, and great as Jehovah or Moses. History was once upon a time, it had once been present and real, it had hurled its thunders and lightnings and long since passed away; now it was remote and venerable, framed in books, and studied in school. The most recent episode in history brought to the cognizance of us schoolboys was the War of 1870. This was more surprising and more exciting than the rest, for our fathers and uncles had taken part in it and we ourselves had only missed it by a few years. How glorious it must have been: heroism, waving flags, generals on horseback, a newly elected emperor. As we were solemnly—and credibly—assured, miracles and deeds of heroism had been performed in that war, the whole thing had been magnificent and genuinely "historical"—quite different from yesterday and today. Men and women had performed amazing deeds, suffered amazing hardships; the people all together had wept and laughed, swept off their feet by the heady events; strangers had embraced one another on the street; bravery and self-sacrifice had been self-evident. Heavens above! To have witnessed such times! None of the people we knew were heroes, neither the teachers

(61

who at certain times of year told us those inspiring stories nor our fathers and uncles, so many of whom had fought in that great, heroic war. But there must have been something in it, there were thick illustrated books, Bismarck's picture hung in every living room, and each autumn Sedan Day was celebrated, the greatest holiday in the year.

Not until I was fifteen did this glow begin to pale for me. Then I began to doubt the venerable character of history, I refused to believe any longer that the men and nations of earlier times were different from those of today, that their lives had consisted not of everyday events but of scenes from grand opera. I knew it was our teachers' duty to crush us as much as possible; they demanded virtues of us which they themselves did not possess, the history they set before us was a hoax devised by grownups in order to belittle us and keep us in our places.

If I conceived such a frivolous, disrespectful view of history, there were reasons. Young people do not live by criticism or negations but by feelings and ideals. And something was stirring inside me that has persisted ever since: I was becoming distrustful of voices from outside, and the more official they were, the more I distrusted them. All in all, I was beginning to feel that what is really interesting and worthwhile, what can truly concern us, excite us, and give us fulfillment, is not outside us but within us. Of course I didn't know this was true—but I felt it, and I began to read philosophy, to become a freethinker, to burrow my way into the poets—always with the obscure presentiment that this was my way, the way to myself, and that no other way was right for me or what I needed. I embarked on what Christians call "meditation" and psychoanalysts "introversion." I cannot say whether this way, this way of being and living, is better than any other; all I know is that for a religious man or a poet it is necessary, and that even if they want to and try very hard they will never become adept at what the official purveyors of wisdom of our day call "thinking historically."

For many years I was able to let the world run its course and conversely. For me what was taken seriously in the world and featured in speeches and editorials was mere sound and fury—while to the world what I did, what I took seriously and held sacred, was play and fancy. And this might have gone on. But then suddenly history turned up again! Suddenly editorialists, university professors, and high-school teachers proclaimed that once again history had crowded out everyday life, that a "great day" had dawned. We unworldly souls, writers and others, who shrugged our shoulders at history, and we men of religious mind, who warned our fellow citizens of the insane arrogance and terrifying insouciance of our leaders, were no longer harmless poets, objects of ridicule— we had become antipatriots, defeatists, and bellyachers, to cite only a few of the lovely new terms. We were denounced, we were blacklisted, we were deluged with venomous articles in the "right-thinking" press. We fared no better in our private lives. When in the spring of 1915 I asked a German friend what would be so dreadful about returning Alsace to France under certain circumstances, he observed that he personally forgave me my foibles but that I had better not say such things to anyone else if I wanted to keep my skull intact.

Everyone was still talking about the "greatness of the

times," and I still failed to see it. Of course I understand why these times seemed great to a good many people. Thousands made their first contact with the soul, with some kind of inner life. Old maids who had been feeding poodles were caring for the wounded; in risking their lives, young men gained their first overpowering feeling of what life is. This is not to be sneezed at, there was a greatness in it—but only for those who thought historically and could speak of great times and paltry times. For the rest of us, the poets and religious-minded, who believed in God even on weekdays and were already familiar with the life of the soul, to us these times seemed no greater or less great than any others. Because, in our innermost heart and being, we lived outside the times.

And we feel the same way now that history is back on the playbill and grand opera is again being performed on the world stage. Much has been done that we ourselves desired—powers we regarded as diabolical have fallen, men whom we detested as evil and dangerous have left the scene.

And yet we are still unable to throw ourselves wholly into great events, to share in the intoxication of these new "great times." We feel the trembling of the earth, we share in the suffering of the victims, the poverty and the hunger, but neither in these sufferings nor in the red flags, new republics, and popular enthusiasms do we see true "greatness." Even today the one reality that we recognize and take a wholehearted interest in is the vital force in history, the flaring up of the divine. The Kaiser was our enemy, and yet we should have felt profound sympathy for him if he had managed to abdicate in a great and worthy manner. We feel infinitely more love for the young soldier who went to his death with the wildest, blindest delusions about Fatherland and Emperor and regard him as infinitely more important than the intelligent democratic orator who calls him a fool. Democracy or monarchy, federal republic or federation of republics are all the same to us; what interests us is not the what but the how. We prefer a madman, who does a mad thing with his whole heart, to the professors who can be expected to kowtow to the new regime as spinelessly as yesterday they bowed down to princes and altars. We are all for a "transvaluation of all values"—but such a transvaluation can only be effected in our own hearts.

I hear the voices of those who attribute our ahistorical, nonpolitical attitude to the blasé indifference of "intellectuals." They take us for penpushers, for whom war and revolution, death and life are mere words. Undoubtedly there are such men. But they have nothing in common with us. We are not unprincipled. True, we do not recognize "good" and "bad," right or left principles—but we distinguish two varieties of human being: those who try to live by their principles and those who carry them in their vest pockets. We do not regard as a shining example the German who, because he is faithful to the Kaiser and unable to live in a revolutionized world, takes his life in a spirit of romantic chivalry at the foot of a statue of William II; but we love him and understand him, whereas we despise the clever man who has already learned to speak the revolutionary jargon as fluently as he formerly spoke the old patriotic jargon.

What mighty things are happening today, how many hearts are beating once again with passionate devotion and hope! How immense are the possibilities! We eccentrics and preachers in the desert do not stand aloof, we are not indifferent, we do not look down from above— but to us, only what happens in human souls seems great. To us the conversion from faith in the Kaiser to demo- cratic faith is in itself a mere change of flags. We wish that for many thousands of men it might be more!

Nowhere has the end of a four years' war, marked only recently by the armistice on the western front, been cele- brated. The celebrations have been on this side for the end of despotism, on the other side for victory. No one seems greatly excited over the fact that after four years of horror the senseless shooting has stopped. Strange world! Over what trifles, by comparison, people have started in once again to smash windowpanes and each other's skulls!

The Reich
December 1918

THERE WAS ONCE a large and beautiful country, but
it was not rich. The people were upright, strong, and
able, but undemanding and contented with their lot.
There was little conspicuous wealth, lavish living, or public display, and not infrequently the large country's
wealthier neighbors cast looks of mockery or mocking
commiseration upon its unassuming people.

Yet certain things that cannot be bought for money but
are prized by humankind throve among this otherwise
inglorious people. They throve so well that in course of
time the country though poor came to be held in high
esteem. Such things throve as music, literature, and
thought. A great philosopher, priest, or poet is under no
obligation to be rich and fashionably dressed or to shine
in society, he is honored for what he is, and that is the
attitude the more powerful nations took toward this
strange poor nation. They shrugged their shoulders at its
poverty and its rather awkward bearing in the world, but
they praised its thinkers, poets, and musicians and spoke
of them without envy.

So it came to pass that though this land of thought
remained poor and was often oppressed by its neighbors,
it poured forth a steady, quiet stream of warmth and
thoughtfulness, which inspired its neighbors and the
whole world.

But from time immemorial this people had been marked by a striking characteristic, which not only aroused the ridicule of foreigners but was also a source of bitter anguish at home: its many different branches had always been at odds with each other, torn by quarrels and jealousies. From time to time the country's outstanding men suggested that the various branches should unite in friendship and common effort, but the thought that one branch or its prince might rise above the rest and assume leadership was so repugnant to the others that no agreement was ever arrived at.

A victory was won over a foreign prince and conqueror who had grievously oppressed the country and it seemed for a time as though this might lead to unification. But soon the old quarrels were resumed; the princelings were recalcitrant, and their subjects had received so many favors from them in the form of posts, titles, and colored ribbons that by and large they were contented and disinclined to innovation.

Meanwhile, the whole world was going through a great change, that strange transformation of men and things which had risen like a specter or an epidemic from the smoke of the first steam engines to turn all life on its head. The world was filled with toil, governed by machines which drove men to work harder and harder. Great riches were produced; the continent that had invented the machines gained even greater power than before over the world as a whole, its most powerful nations divided the other continents among them, and those that were not powerful were left empty-handed.

The expansionist wave spread to the country we have been speaking of, but it was weak and its share in the spoils was small. The wealth of the world seemed to have been redistributed, and again the poor country seemed to have got the short end.

Then suddenly events took a new course. The voices that had clamored for unification had never fallen silent. A great and powerful statesman made his appearance, a brilliant victory over a neighboring people strengthened and unified the country, the branches of the people joined hands and established a great Reich. The poor country of dreamers, thinkers, and musicians had awakened. Rich, powerful, and united, it became the equal of its powerful elder brothers. There was little more to be pillaged and seized on distant continents; the new power found that the prizes had all been taken. But now machine civilization, which had scarcely touched that country up until then, entered on a spectacular development. The whole country and its people underwent a headlong transformation. They grew rich, they grew powerful and feared. They accumulated wealth and surrounded themselves with a threefold defensive wall of soldiers, cannon, and forts. Soon the neighboring states grew alarmed and they too, spurred by fear and distrust of the newcomer, took to building palisades, cannon, and warships.

But that was not the worst. Both sides could afford these staggering armaments, and no one thought of a war; they were arming just to be on the safe side, because rich people like to see iron walls around their money.

Far worse was what was happening inside the Reich. This people which for so long had been half mocked, half admired by the world, which had possessed so much culture and so little money, now awoke to the charms of money and power. They built and saved, they traded and loaned money, and no one could get rich quickly enough. The owner of a mill or smithy suddenly needed a factory, the employer, of three journeymen needed twenty, and some were soon employing hundreds or thousands. And the faster all the many hands and machines worked, the faster the money piled up—in the hands of those who had the knack of piling up money. But the many many workers ceased to be the familiars and companions of a master craftsman and sank into bondage and slavery.

The same happened in other countries; there too the workshop became a factory, the master craftsman became a monarch, the worker a slave. No country in the world was spared this fate. What distinguished the young Reich was that its founding coincided with the emergence in the world of the new spirit of business enterprise. The Reich had no past behind it, no long-accumulated wealth; it raced into the new fast-moving times like an impatient child.

True, voices were raised in warning. They told the people that this was the wrong path and recalled the olden times, the quiet unassuming glory of their country, the spiritual mission that had once guided it, the steady stream of noble ideas, music, and poetry which it had formerly sent out into the world. But in their joy over their new wealth, the people laughed. The earth was round and revolved; it was all very well that their grandfathers had written poems and books of philosophy, but the new generation was going to show that their country was capable of something else. And so they hammered away in their thousands of factories and made new machines, new railroads, new commodities, and, just to be on the safe side, new rifles and cannon. The rich became divorced from the people, the poor workers found themselves forsaken, and they too stopped thinking of the people, of which they were a part, and took to thinking only of themselves, their own needs and desires. And the wealthy and powerful, who had acquired so many cannon and rifles as a precaution against external enemies, congratulated themselves on their foresight, for now they had enemies within, who were perhaps even more dangerous.

All this culminated in the Great War which for years so devastated the world. Today we stand among its ruins, still deafened by its noise, embittered by its absurdity, and sickened by the streams of blood that haunt all our dreams.

And the outcome of the war was that the thriving young Reich, whose sons had rushed into battle with such enthusiasm, collapsed. It was defeated, terribly defeated. And before they would even discuss peace, the victors demanded heavy tribute of the vanquished people. For days on end, as the defeated army flocked homeward, the symbols of the country's former power were transported in the opposite direction, to be surrendered to the victorious enemy. Machines and money flowed from the defeated country into the hands of the enemy.

Yet, in the moment of its greatest affliction, the defeated people had come to its senses. It had driven out its leaders and princes and declared itself to be of age. It had set up councils of its own members and proclaimed its will to face up to its misfortune with its own mind and its own energies.

This people that has come of age amid such bitter trials does not yet know where it is going or where to seek help and leadership. But the gods know, and they know why they visited the miseries of war on this people and on the world.

Out of the darkness of these days a light beckons, showing the path that this defeated people must travel.

It cannot return to childhood. No one can do that. It cannot simply give away its cannon, its machines, and its money, and go back to writing poems and playing sonatas in peaceful little cities. But it can take the path which an individual must take when his life has led him into error and deep torment. It can recollect its past, its origin and childhood, its greatness, its glory and its defeat, and through this recollection find the strength which is inherent in it and can never be lost. As the pious say, it must "look within." And deep within itself it will find intact its own innermost being, which will not try to evade its destiny but embrace it and, building on what is best and most essential in itself, make a fresh start.

If this happens and if this hard-pressed nation willingly and honestly travels the path of destiny, something of what was will be reborn. Once again a steady quiet stream will flow out into the world from this people, and once again those who were its enemies will listen with emotion to the murmurings of this quiet stream.

The Path of Love
December 1918

AS LONG AS A MAN IS WELL OFF, he can afford to do
superfluous and foolish things. When well-being
gives way to affliction, life begins to educate us. When a
misbehaved child resists punishment and correction on
the ground that other children are equally misbehaved,
we smile and know the answer. But we Germans have
been just such misbehaved children. Throughout the war
we kept saying that our enemies, to say the least, were no
better than we were. When accused of expansionism, we
pointed to England's colonies. In response to critics of our
autocratic state, we said that President Wilson held more
absolute power than any German prince. And so on.

The days of affliction have come. May they bring with
them a beginning of education! We Germans are very
badly off, we do not know how we shall live tomorrow, if
at all. Now more than ever we are under great temptation
to indulge in useless gestures and feelings. We read letters and poems, articles and comments that speculate on
all the evil instincts of a punished child. Here and there
Germans are beginning once again to think "historically"
(that is, inhumanly). Our present situation is likened to
the situation to which we reduced France in 1870, and
the same inferences are drawn as were then drawn in
France: grit your teeth, endure what must be endured,

but in your hearts nurture the vengeance which at some later day will repair the disaster!

When four years ago, in the first flush of war, German soldiers wrote on their barracks gates: "Declarations of war still accepted," those of us who thought differently were powerless to speak. For every word of humanity, of warning, every word expressing a serious thought for the future, each one of us was rewarded with vilification and suspicion, persecution and loss of friendships.

We don't want that to happen again. We know now that our psychology was wrong, that at the beginning of the war we made gestures and uttered words that had their source, not in an authentic will, but in hysteria. True, the "others" did the same; the insults heaped on the enemy, even on his noblest qualities and supranational achievements, were just as ignoble in the opposing camp as here in Germany; on both sides there were evil demagogues who spoke hysterically and irresponsibly.

One thing we must finally stop doing is justifying ourselves by the argument that the enemy behaved no better. If today General Foch is as relentless as our able General Hoffman was in Brest-Litovsk, it ill becomes us to howl at him. He is behaving like a victor, just as we behaved like victors.

Today we are not victors. Our role has changed. And whether we are able to go on living in the world and to prosper depends entirely on our ability to recognize our role, on our sincere willingness to bear the consequences of our situation.

Affliction has moved our people to get rid of their old leaders and declare themselves sovereign. Like every authentic action, this action welled from the fertile depths

of the unconscious. It was an awakening from profound
illusions. It was a breach with sclerotic tradition. It was
the first glimmer of an insight: "Since the national ideals
of our old leaders were a fraud, aren't humanity, reason,
and good will the better way?"

Our hearts said yes. From one day to the next we have
lost the "most sacred treasures" of the old days; we threw
them away because we saw that they were no better than
painted costume jewelry.

We must continue in this spirit. We have chosen the
hardest path a man, not to say a people, can travel: the
path of sincerity, the path of love. If we travel it to the
end, we shall have won. Then this long war and painful
defeat shall cease to be a festering wound and become
our deserved good fortune, our better future, our pride
and possession.

The path of love is so hard to travel because there is so
little faith in love, because it meets with distrust on every
hand. Of this we too are made aware as we start on our
new path. Our enemies say: You have taken refuge under
the red flag in order to evade the consequences of your
actions!—But words cannot convince the enemy of our
sincerity. We must win him over slowly and irresistibly
with truth and love. Good ideas are in the air—the brotherhood of man, a League of Nations, friendly cooperation
among all peoples, disarmament—there has been much
talk of them both here and in the enemy countries, some
of it not very serious. We must take these ideas seriously
and do everything in our power to implement them.

Ours is the role and the task of the vanquished. The
task is the sacred and immemorial task of all the unfortunate on earth: not only to bear our lot but to assume it

completely, to make ourselves one with it, to understand it—until our misfortune is no longer felt to be an alien fate, hailed down upon us from distant clouds, but becomes part and parcel of ourselves, permeating our being and guiding our thoughts.

Many of us are held back from such full acceptance of our fate (the only means of transcending it) by false shame. We have grown accustomed to demanding something of ourselves that no man has in himself by nature: heroism. As long as you are winning, heroism seems very attractive. Once you are defeated and require the strength to face your situation and to master it, heroism proves to be a hostile, dangerous, and paralyzing force— then it is unmasked as the Moloch it is. This Moloch, who has cost us so many of our brothers, this mad god who has now ruled the world for years, must no longer be our ideal and our leader!

No, we must travel the path we have started out on, the hard lonely path of sincerity and love, to its end. For never again must we revert to what we were: a powerful people with a great deal of money and many cannon, governed by money and cannon. Even if it offered an opportunity to recover all our old power and establish world hegemony, we must not take that path again, or even flirt with the thought of it. To do so would be to renounce everything which, prompted by deep affliction and desperate self-knowledge, we have done and begun to do in the past few weeks. If our revolution has been a mere attempt to get off easier, to shirk some part of our fate, then this revolution is worthless.

That must not be! No, this magnificent, involuntary, sudden, and powerful movement was not born of shrewd calculations, it came from the heart, from millions of hearts. And now let what came from the heart be carried on with a forthright heart! Let us resist the temptation of theatrical, hysterical heroisms; let us not clothe ourselves in the bitterness of unjustly chastised victims, and in particular let us not persist in denying the right of those who have set themselves up as our judges to judge us. Whether our enemies are worthy of this terrible right or not is irrelevant. Fate comes from God, and unless we learn to recognize it as holy and wise, unless we learn to love it and fulfill it, we shall have been truly defeated. Then we shall no longer be the noble vanquished, capable of bearing what cannot be averted, but disgraceful failures.

Sincerity is a good thing, but it is worthless without love. Love is self-mastery, the power to understand, the ability to smile in sorrow. Love of ourselves and our fate, fervent acceptance of what the Inscrutable has in store for us, even when we cannot fathom and understand it— that is our goal. Later on perhaps the peoples of Russia and Austria will join us on our path—for the present we need only the will and decision to carry on as we have started.

And out of our will to fulfill our fate, to be ready and willing for the new, out of our trust in the simple eloquence of our affliction, our suffering humanity, a hundred new energies will grow. Once one has assumed the whole of one's fate, one's eyes are opened to the particulars. The "good will" of the ancient promise will help our poor to bear their poverty, will help our industrialists to convert from self-seeking capitalism to the selfless administration of human effort. Such good will will enable our future ambassadors abroad to replace the old hypocritical busyness with a new and creditable defense of the interests of our people as a whole. It will speak from the mouths of our poets and artists and from all our endeavor; slowly and quietly but profoundly, it will win for us what we have lost in our dealings with the world: confidence and love.

Self-will

1919

T HERE IS ONE VIRTUE that I love, and only one. I
call it self-will. —I cannot bring myself to think
so highly of all the many virtues we read about in books
and hear about from our teachers. True, all the virtues
man has devised for himself might be subsumed under a
single head: obedience. But the question is: *whom* are we
to obey? For self-will is also obedience. But all the other
virtues, the virtues that are so highly esteemed and
praised, consist in obedience to manmade laws. Self-will
is the only virtue that takes no account of these laws. A
self-willed man obeys a different law, the one law I hold
absolutely sacred—the law in himself, his own "will."

It is a great pity that self-will should be held in such
low esteem! Do men think well of it? Oh no, they regard
it as a vice or at best as a deplorable aberration. They call
it by its eloquent full name only where it arouses antagonism and hatred. (Come to think of it, true virtues always
arouse antagonism and hatred. Witness Socrates, Jesus,
Giordano Bruno, and all other self-willed men.) When
anyone is in some measure inclined to evaluate self-will
as a virtue or at least as an estimable quality, he gives it a
more acceptable name. "Character" or "personality"
doesn't sound as crude, not to say sinful, as "self-will";
"originality" will do in a pinch, though only in connection

with tolerated eccentrics, artists and such. In art, where self-will represents no discernible threat to capital and society, it is highly prized under the name of originality; indeed, a certain self-will is regarded as positively desirable in artists and rewarded with high prices. In other contexts, however, the language of our day employs the words "character" or "personality" for a very odd phenomenon, to wit, something which can be exhibited and decorated but which on every halfway important occasion is very careful to bow to the laws of society. A man who has a few notions and opinions of his own but does not live in accordance with them is said to have character. He intimates in subtle ways that he thinks differently, that he has ideas of his own. In this mild form, hardly separable from vanity, character is regarded as a virtue even in a man's own lifetime. But if a man has ideas of his own and actually lives by them, he loses his favorable "character" certificate and is said to be merely "self-willed." But suppose we take the word literally. What does self-willed mean? It means "having a will of one's own."

Everything on earth, every single thing, has its will. Every stone, every blade of grass, every flower, every shrub, every animal grows, lives, moves, and feels in accordance with its "self-will," and that is why the world is good, rich, and beautiful. If there are flowers and fruits, oaks and birches, horses and chickens, tin and iron, gold and coal, it is because every thing, great and small, bears within itself its own "will," its own law, and follows this law surely and unswervingly.

There are only two poor accursed beings on earth who are excluded from following this eternal call and from being, growing, living, and dying as an inborn and deeply ingrained self-will commands. Only man and the domestic animals he has tamed are condemned to obey, not the law of life and growth, but other laws that are made by men and from time to time broken and changed by men. And the strangest part of it is that those few who have disregarded these arbitrary laws to follow their own natural law have come to be revered as heroes and liberators —though most of them were persecuted in their lifetime. The same mankind which praises obedience to its arbitrary laws as the supreme virtue of the living reserves its eternal pantheon for those who have defied those laws and preferred to die rather than betray their "self-will."

"Tragedy," that sublime, mystic, and sacred word descended from the mythical youth of man and so monstrously abused by our journalists, signifies the fate of the hero who meets his doom because he follows his own star in opposition to the traditional laws. Through tragic heroes and through them alone man has time and time again gained insight into his inner being, his "self-will." Time and time again a tragic hero, a self-willed man, has shown the millions of common men, of cowards, that disobedience to the decrees of man is not gross irresponsibility but fidelity to a far higher, sacred law. In other words: the human herd instinct demands adaptation and subordination—but for his highest honors man elects not the meek, the pusillanimous, the supine, but precisely the self-willed men, the heroes.

Just as reporters abuse the language when they term some senseless accident "tragic" (which for those clowns is synonymous with "deplorable"), it is an abuse of language to say—as is now fashionable, especially among stay-at-homes—that our poor soldiers, slaughtered at the front, died a "heroic death." That is sentimentality. Of course the soldiers who died in the war are worthy of our deepest sympathy. Many of them did great things and suffered greatly, and in the end they paid with their lives. But that does not make them "heroes." The common soldier, at whom an officer bellows as he would at a dog, is not suddenly transformed into a hero by the bullet that kills him. To suppose that there can be millions of "heroes" is in itself an absurdity.

The obedient well-behaved citizen who does his duty is not a "hero." Only an *individual* who has fashioned his "self-will," his noble, natural inner law, into his destiny can be a hero. "Destiny and cast of mind are words for the same thing," said Novalis, one of the profoundest and least-known German thinkers. But only a hero finds the courage to fulfill his destiny.

If the majority of men possessed this courage and self-will, the earth would be a different place. No, say our paid teachers (the same who are so adept at praising the heroes and self-willed men of former times), everything would be topsy-turvy. But in reality life would be richer and better if each man independently followed his own law and will. In such a world, it is true, some of the insults and unreflecting blows that keep our venerable judges so busy today might go unpunished. Now and then a murderer might go free—but doesn't that happen now in spite of all our laws and punishments? On the other hand, many of the terrible, unspeakably sad, and insane things that we witness today in our so well-ordered world would be unknown and impossible. Such as wars between nations.

Now I hear the authorities saying: "You preach revolution."

Wrong again. Such a mistake is possible only among herd men. I preach self-will, not revolution. How could I want a revolution? Revolution is war; like all other war, it is a "prolongation of politics by other means." But a man who has once felt the courage to be himself, who has heard the voice of his own destiny, cares nothing for politics, whether it be monarchist or democratic, revolutionary or conservative! He is concerned with something else. His self-will, like the profound, magnificent, God-given self-will that inhabits every blade of grass, has no other aim than his own growth. "Egoism," if you will. But very different from the sordid egoism of those who lust for money or power!

A man endowed with the "self-will" I have in mind does not seek money or power. He despises them, but not because he is a paragon of virtue or a resigned altruist. Far from it! The truth is simply that money, power, and all the possessions for which men torment and ultimately shoot each other mean little to one who has come to himself, to a self-willed man. He values only one thing, the mysterious power in himself which bids him live and helps him to grow. This power can be neither preserved nor increased nor deepened by money and power, because money and power are the inventions of distrust. Those who distrust the life-giving force within them, or who have none, are driven to compensate through such substitutes as money. When a man has confidence in himself, when all he wants in the world is to live out his destiny in freedom and purity, he comes to regard all those vastly overestimated and far too costly possessions as mere accessories, pleasant perhaps to have and make use of, but never essential.

How I love the virtue of self-will! Once you have learned to treasure it and discovered some parcel of it in yourself, all the most highly commended virtues become strangely questionable.

Patriotism is one of these. I have nothing against it. For the individual it substitutes a larger complex. But it is truly prized as a virtue only in time of war—that naïve and absurdly inadequate means of "prolonging politics." The soldier who kills enemies is always regarded as a greater patriot than the peasant who tills his land to the best of his ability. Because the peasant derives advantage from what he does. And in our strange system of morality a virtue that is useful or profitable to its possessor is always held in suspicion.

Why? Because we are accustomed to seek profit at the cost of others. Because, distrustful as we are, we are always obliged to covet what belongs to someone else.

The savage believes that the vital force of the enemy he kills passes into him. All war, competition, and mistrust among men seem to spring from just such a primitive belief. We should be happier if we looked upon the poor peasant as at least the soldier's equal! If we could overcome our superstitious belief that the life or joy of life acquired by any man or people must necessarily be taken away from another man or people!

But now I hear our friend the teacher: "That sounds all very well, but now I must ask you to consider the matter objectively, from the economic standpoint! World production is . . ."

To which I reply: "No, thank you. The economic

standpoint isn't the least bit objective, it is a glass through which one can see all sorts of things. Before the war, for example, economic considerations were invoked to prove that a world war was impossible or that if one did break out it could not last long. Today, again on economic grounds, I can prove the opposite. No, let's forget such fantasies for once and think in terms of realities!"

None of these "standpoints," whatever we may wish to call them and whatever the girth of the professor who professes them, gets us anywhere. They all offer uncertain ground. We are not adding machines or any other kind of machines. For a man there is only *one* natural standpoint, only *one* natural criterion. And that is self-will. The destiny of the self-willed man can be neither capitalism nor socialism, neither England nor America; his only living destiny is the silent, ungainsayable law in his own heart, which comfortable habits make it so hard to obey but which to the self-willed man is destiny and godhead.

Zarathustra's Return
A WORD TO GERMAN YOUTH
1919

There was once a German spirit, a German courage, a German manhood that did not express themselves in the uproar of the herd or in mass enthusiasm. The last great vehicle of that spirit was Nietzsche, who, amid the business boom and sheeplike conformism that characterized the beginnings of the German Empire, became an antipatriot and anti-German. In this little book I wish to remind the young German intellectuals of that man, of his courage and solitude, and in so doing turn their minds away from the herd outcry (whose present whining tone is not a jot more pleasant than the brutal, bullying tone it assumed in those "great days") to a few simple facts and experiences of the soul. With regard to nation and collectivity, let every man act as his needs and conscience dictate—but if in the process he loses himself, his own soul, whatever he does will be worthless. Only a few men in our impoverished and defeated Germany have begun to recognize that weeping and complaining are fruitless, and to gird themselves like men for the future. Only a few suspect how deeply the German mind had degenerated long before the war. If we wish once again

*to have minds and men capable of securing our
future, we must not begin at the tail end, with political methods and forms of government, but at the
beginning, with the building of the personality.
That is the subject of my little book. It first appeared
anonymously in Switzerland (where it went into
several printings), because I did not wish to arouse
the young people's distrust with a familiar name.
I wanted them to consider it without prejudice, and
that they did. Accordingly, I have no further ground
for remaining anonymous.*

Hermann Hesse's preface
to the first signed edition

WHEN THE RUMOR went round among the young
people in the capital that Zarathustra had reap-
peared and had been seen here and there in the streets and
squares, a few young men went out to look for him. These
were young men who had returned home from the war
and were seized with anguish amid the change and upheaval of their homeland, for they saw that great things
were happening, but the meaning of these things was obscure and to many they were without rhyme or reason. In
former years all these young men had looked upon
Zarathustra as their prophet and guide; they had read
what is written concerning him with the enthusiasm of
youth; they had spoken and thought about him on their
wanderings over heath and mountain, and at night in the
lamplight of their rooms. And because the voice that first
and most forcefully turns a man's thoughts to his own self

and his own fate is held sacred, they had held Zarathustra sacred.

The young men found Zarathustra in a wide street filled with people. He was standing pressed against a wall, listening to a demagogue who was haranguing the crowd from the top of a vehicle. Zarathustra listened, smiled, and looked into the faces of the people. He looked into those faces as an aged hermit looks into the waves of the sea or the clouds at morning. He saw the fear; he saw the impatience and the perplexed, plaintive, childlike anxiety; he saw the courage and hatred in the eyes of the resolute and despairing. And he did not weary of looking, while at the same time listening to the speaker. The young men recognized him by his smile. He was neither old nor young, he looked neither like a teacher nor like a soldier, he looked like a man—like man himself when he first rose out of the darkness of the beginning, the first of his kind.

And yet, after doubting for a time that it was he, they recognized him by his smile. His smile was bright but not kindly; it was guileless, but not good-natured. It was the smile of a warrior, but still more the smile of an old man who has seen much and has ceased to set store by tears.

When the speech was at an end and the people began, amid a great uproar, to disperse, the young men approached Zarathustra and greeted him with reverence.

"Master, you are here," they stammered; "at last in our day of greatest affliction, you have returned. Welcome, Zarathustra! You will tell us what to do, you will lead us. You will save us from this greatest of all perils."

Smiling, he bade them accompany him, and when they had started off he said: "I am in very good spirits, my

Zarathustra's Return

friends. I have returned, perhaps for a day, perhaps for an hour, and I see you play-acting. It has always been a pleasure to me to watch people play-acting. They are never so honest as then."

The young men heard him and exchanged glances; they thought there was too much mockery, too much levity, too much unconcern in Zarathustra's words. How could he speak of play-acting when his people were in misery? How could he smile and be so cheerful when his country had been defeated and was facing ruin? How could all this, the people and the public speaker, the gravity of the hour, their own solemnity and veneration— how could all this be a mere spectacle to him, merely something to observe and smile at? Should he not, at such a time, shed bitter tears, lament and rend his garments? And, most of all, was it not time, high time, to act? To do great deeds? To set an example? To save his country and people from certain doom?

"I see, my young friends," said Zarathustra, who divined their unspoken thoughts, "that you are displeased with me. I expected as much, and yet you surprise me. Such expectations always go hand in hand with their contrary; one part of us expects something, another part hopes for the opposite. That, my friends, is how I feel now. —But come now, you wished to speak with Zarathustra, did you not?"

"Yes! Yes, indeed!" they cried eagerly.

Then Zarathustra smiled and said: "Well then, my dear friends, speak with Zarathustra, hear Zarathustra. The man who stands before you is not a demagogue, or a soldier, or a king, or a general; he is Zarathustra, the old hermit and joker, inventor of the last laugh, and of so

(89

many other sad last things. From me, my friends, you
cannot learn how to govern nations and repair defeats. I
cannot teach you how to drive herds or appease the hungry. Those are not Zarathustra's arts. Those are not
Zarathustra's concerns."

The young men were silent and a look of disappointment passed over their faces. Dejected and disgruntled,
they walked beside the prophet and for a long time found
no words with which to answer him. At length one of
them, the youngest, spoke; and his eyes flashed as he
spoke, and Zarathustra looked upon him with pleasure.

"Then tell us," began the youngest of the young men,
"tell us what you have to say. For if you have only come
to mock us and to mock the affliction of your people, we
have better things to do than to walk about with you,
listening to your excellent jokes. Look at us, Zarathustra.
All of us, young as we are, have fought in the war and
looked death in the face; and we are in no mood for
games and amusing pastimes. We revered you, O master,
and loved you, but greater than our love for you is our
love for ourselves and our people. We want you to know
that."

Zarathustra's countenance brightened when he heard
the young man speak, and he looked with kindness, nay,
tenderness, into his angry eyes.

"My friend," he said with his best smile, "how right you
are not to accept old Zarathustra sight unseen, to sound
him out, and to tickle him in what you take to be his
vulnerable spot. How right you are, my dear boy, to be
mistrustful! Moreover, I must tell you, you have just
spoken excellent words, the kind of words Zarathustra
likes to hear. Did you not say: 'We love ourselves more

than we love Zarathustra'? Such forthrightness goes straight to my heart! With those words you have baited me, slippery old fish that I am; soon you will have me dangling from your hook!"

At that moment shouts, loud cries, and tumult were heard from far off; it sounded strange and absurd in the quiet evening. And when Zarathustra saw the eyes and thoughts of his young companions darting in that direction like young hares, he changed his tone. Suddenly his voice sounded as though it came from a strange, remote place—it sounded just as it had when the young men had first come to know him, like a voice that comes not from men but from stars or gods or, still more, like the voice that every man hears secretly in his own heart at times when God is in him.

The friends harkened, their thoughts and senses returned to Zarathustra, for now they recognized the voice that had once burst upon their early youth like the voice of an unknown God.

"Hear me, my children," he said earnestly, addressing himself chiefly to the youngest. "If you wish to hear a bell tone, you must not strike upon tin. And if you wish to play the flute, you must not set your lips to a wineskin. Do you understand me, my friends? Think back, my dear friends, think back and remember: what was it that you learned from your Zarathustra in those hours of enthusiasm? What was it? Was it wisdom for the counting house, or for the street, or for the battlefield? Did I give you advice for kings, did I speak to you like a king, or a citizen, or a politician, or a merchant? No, if you recall, I spoke like Zarathustra, I spoke my language, I stood before you like a mirror, in which to see yourselves. Did you ever "learn something" from me? Was I ever a language teacher or a teacher of any other subject? No, Zarathustra is not a teacher, you cannot ask him questions and learn from him, and jot down big and little formulas to be used as the need arises. Zarathustra is a man, he is you and I. Zarathustra is the man for whom you are searching in yourselves, the forthright, unseduced man—how could he wish to seduce you? Zarathustra has seen much and suffered much, he has cracked many nuts and been bitten by many snakes. But he has learned only one thing, he prides himself only on one bit of wisdom. He has learned to be Zarathustra. And that is what you want to learn from him, yet so often lack the courage to learn. You must learn to be yourselves, just as I have learned to be Zarathustra. You must unlearn the habit of being someone else or nothing at all, of imitating the voices of others and mistaking the faces of others for your own. —Therefore, my friends, when Zarathustra speaks to you, look for no wisdom, no arts, no formulas, no Pied Piper's tricks in his words; look for the man himself. From a stone you can learn what hardness is, from a bird what it is to sing. And from me you can learn what man and destiny are."

Thus conversing, they had come to the edge of the city, and for a long while they walked together in the evening, under the rustling trees. They asked him many questions, often they laughed with him and often they despaired of him. And one of them wrote down what Zarathustra said to them that evening, or some part of it, and preserved it for his friends.

This is what he wrote as he recollected Zarathustra and his words:

OF DESTINY

So spake Zarathustra to us:

One thing is given to man which makes him into a god, which reminds him that he is a god: to know destiny.

What makes me Zarathustra is that I have come to know Zarathustra's destiny. That I have lived his life. Few men know their destiny. Few men live their lives. Learn to live your lives! Learn to know your destiny!

You have been lamenting so much over the destiny of your people. But a destiny we lament over is not yet ours; it is an alien, hostile destiny, an alien god and evil idol, a destiny flung at us like a poisoned arrow out of the darkness.

Learn that destiny does not come from idols; then at last you will know that there are no idols or gods! As a child grows in a woman's womb, so destiny grows in each man's body, or if you will you may say: in his mind or soul. They are the same thing.

And just as the woman is one with her child and loves it beyond all else in the world—so must you learn to love your destiny beyond all else in the world. It must be your god, for you yourselves must be your gods.

When destiny comes to a man from outside, it lays him low, just as an arrow lays a deer low. When destiny comes to a man from within, from his innermost being, it makes him strong, it makes him into a god. It made Zarathustra into Zarathustra—it must make you into yourself!

A man who has recognized his destiny never tries to change it. The endeavor to change destiny is a childish pursuit that makes men quarrel and kill one another. Your emperor and generals tried to change destiny, and so did you. Now that you have failed to change destiny, it has a bitter taste and you look upon it as poison. If you had not tried to change it, if you had taken it to heart as your child, if you had made it into your very own selves, how sweet it would taste! All sorrow, poison, and death are alien, imposed destiny. But every true act, everything that is good and joyful and fruitful on earth, is lived destiny, destiny that has become self.

Before your long war, you were too rich, my friends, you and your fathers were too rich and fat and glutted, and when there was pain in your bellies, you ought to have recognized destiny in your pain and harkened to its good voice. But, children that you were, the pain in your bellies made you angry and you contrived to think that hunger and want were the source of your pain. And so you struck out: to conquer, to gain more space on earth, to acquire more food for your bellies. And now that you have returned home and have not gained what you were after, you have started to moan again, you are beset by all manner of aches and pains; once again you are looking for the wicked, wicked enemy who is responsible for your pain, and you are prepared to shoot him even if he is your brother.

Dear friends, ought you not to consider? Ought you not, just this once, to treat your pain with more respect, more curiosity, more manliness, with less infantile fear and less infantile wailing? Might your bitter pain not be the voice of destiny, might that voice not become sweet once you understand it?

Another thing, my friends. I hear your perpetual lamentations and outcries over the bitter pain and bitter fate that have descended on your people and your fatherland. Forgive me, my friends, if I am just a little distrustful of such pain, just a little reluctant to believe in it! All of you—you and you and you—are you suffering only for your people and fatherland? Where is this fatherland? Where is its head? Where is its heart? Where is the cure to begin? Tell me! Yesterday your fears were for the Kaiser, for the empire that you were so proud of, that you held so sacred. Where is all that today? Your pain did not come from the Kaiser—if it had, would it still be so bitter now that the Kaiser is gone? It did not come from the army or from the fleet or from any conquered province or possession; that is evident to you now. —But why, if you are in pain, must you go on talking about nation and fatherland, about all those great and estimable things which are so easy to talk about but which so easily vanish into thin air? Who is the people? Is it a street speaker or is it those who listen to him; is it those who agree with him or those who brandish their cudgels and shout him down? Do you hear the shooting over there? Where is the people, your people? Is it shooting or being shot at? Is it attacking or being attacked?

You see, it is hard for men to understand each other, and still harder to understand ourselves when we persist in using such big words. If all of you—you and you—are in pain, if you are sick in body or soul, if you are afraid and have a foreboding of danger—why not, if only to amuse yourselves, if only out of curiosity, good healthy curiosity, try to put the question in a different way? Why not ask whether the source of your pain might not be you yourselves? For a brief period in the past you were all convinced that the Russians were your enemy and the root of all evil. A little while later it was the English, and then the French, and then others, and each time you were sure, and each time it was a dismal comedy, ending in misery. But now that you have seen that the pain has its source in ourselves, that we cannot heal it by blaming the enemy—why, once again, do you neglect to look for the source of your pain where it is: within yourselves. Might it not be that what pains you is not the people and not the fatherland and not world hegemony, and not democracy either for that matter, but your own stomach or liver, an ulcer or cancer inside you—and that only a childish fear of the truth and the doctor makes you imagine that you yourself are in perfect health but alas so afflicted by some ailment in your people? Might that not be so? Isn't your curiosity aroused? Might it not be an amusing exercise for each one of you to examine what ails you and try to determine its source?

You might well discover that a third or a half of your pain and then some originates in your own selves, and that it might be a good idea to take cold baths or drink less wine or undertake some other sort of cure, instead of probing and doctoring the fatherland. That, I believe, is quite possible—and wouldn't it be a fine thing? Mightn't something be done about it? Wouldn't there be hope for the future? A hope of transforming pain into profit and poison into destiny?

It strikes you as mean and selfish to forget the fatherland and heal yourselves. But perhaps, my friends, you are not as right as you suppose! Wouldn't you say that a fatherland upon which every sick citizen does not project his own ailments, which hundreds of patients do not try to doctor, might be healthier and more likely to thrive?

Ah, my young friends, you have learned so much in

your young lives! You have been soldiers, you have looked death in the face a hundred times. You are heroes. You are pillars of the fatherland. But I implore you: don't content yourselves with that! Learn more! Strive higher! And remember from time to time what a fine thing integrity is!

ACTION AND SUFFERING

"What ought we to do?" you ask me. You ask me time and time again, and yourselves as well. "Doing"—action— is so important to you, indeed all-important. That is good, my friends, or rather—it would be good, if you fully understood what action is!

But you see, the very question "What ought we to do?" —What action ought we to perform?—this question of an anxious child, shows me how little you know of action.

What you young men call action, I, the old hermit of the mountains, should call by a very different name. I can think of any number of droll or appealing names for this "action" of yours. I should not have to roll it between my fingers very long to turn it neatly and amusingly into its opposite. For it is an opposite. Your "doing" is the opposite of what I call "doing."

No true action, my friends—just listen to the word, listen well, wash your ears with it!—no true action has ever been performed by one who first asked: "What ought I to do?" An action is a light that shines from a good sun. If the sun is not good, if it is not sound and many times tested, or, worse, if it is the kind of sun that asks itself anxiously what it ought to do, it will never shed light. A true action is not the same as "doing something," a true action cannot be cogitated and contrived. Very well, I shall tell you what a true action is. But first, my friends, let me tell you how this action, this "doing," you speak of strikes me. Then we shall understand each other better.

This "action" you wish to perform, which is expected to spring from searching and doubting and meandering— this action, dear friends, is the contrary and mortal enemy of true action. For your action, if you will forgive me an unpleasant word, is cowardice! I see you growing angry, I see in your eyes the look I am so fond of—but wait, hear me out!

You young men are soldiers, and before you were soldiers you, or your fathers, were merchants or manufacturers or the like. Taught in a deplorable school, they and you believed in certain antitheses that were thought to have existed since the beginning of time and to have been created by the gods. These antitheses were your gods. From one of them, the antithesis between man and god, you inferred that a man cannot be a god, and conversely. Zarathustra can find no plainer, simpler way of showing you the dubious and despicable character of those time-honored, sacrosanct antitheses than to open your eyes to the antithesis you so staunchly believe in: that between action and suffering.

Action and suffering, which together make up our lives, are a whole; they are one. A child suffers its begetting, it suffers its birth, its weaning; it suffers here and suffers there until in the end it suffers death. But all the good in a man, for which he is praised or loved, is merely good suffering, the right kind, the living kind of suffering, a suffering to the full. The ability to suffer well is more than half of life—indeed, it is all life. Birth is suffering, growth is suffering, the seed suffers the earth, the root suffers the rain, the bud suffers its flowering.

In the same way, my friends, man suffers destiny. Destiny is earth, it is rain and growth. Destiny hurts.

What you call action is a running-away from pain, a not-wanting-to-be-born, a flight from suffering! You, or your fathers, called it "action" when you bustled about night and day in shops and factories, when you heard many many hammers hammering, when you blew quantities of soot into the air. Don't misunderstand me, I have nothing against your hammers, your soot, or your fathers. But I cannot help smiling when you speak of your bustling as "action." It was not action, it was merely a flight from suffering. It was painful to be alone—and so men established societies. It was painful to hear all manner of voices within you, demanding that you live your own lives, seek your own destiny, die your own death—it was painful, and so you ran away, and made noise with hammers and machines, until the voices receded and fell silent. That is what your fathers did, that is what your teachers did, and that is what you yourselves did. Suffering was demanded of you—and you were indignant, you didn't want to suffer, you wanted only to act! And what did you do? First, in your strange occupations you sacrificed to the god of deafening noise, you were so busy with your activity that you had no time to suffer, to hear, to breathe, to drink the milk of life and the light of heaven. No, you had to be active, perpetually active, perpetually doing. And when the fuss and bustle proved futile, when the destiny within you, instead of ripening into sweetness, decayed and turned to poison, you multiplied your

activity, you created enemies for yourselves, first in your
imagination, then in reality; you went to war, you became
soldiers and heroes. You have made conquests, you have
borne insane hardships and done gigantic deeds. And
now? Are you content? Are your hearts happy and
serene? Is destiny sweet to your taste? No, it is bitterer
than ever, and that is why you are clamoring for more
action, rushing into the streets, storming and shouting,
electing councils, and loading your guns again. All because you are forever in flight from suffering! In flight
from yourselves, from your souls!

I hear your answer. You ask me whether what you have
suffered was not suffering. Was it not suffering when your
brothers died in your arms, when your flesh froze to the
ground or quivered under the surgeon's knife? Yes, all
that was suffering—suffering that you brought upon
yourselves by your own obstinacy, impatient suffering, a
striving to change destiny. It was heroic—insofar as a
man who runs away from destiny, who wants to change
it, can be heroic.

It is hard to learn to suffer. Women succeed more often
and more nobly than men. Learn from them! Learn to
listen when the voice of life speaks! Learn to look when
the sun of destiny plays with your shadows! Learn to
respect life! Learn to respect yourselves!

From suffering springs strength, from suffering springs
health. It is always the "healthy" who suddenly collapse,
who are laid low by a puff of air. Those are the men who
have not learned to suffer. Suffering toughens a man;
suffering tempers him. Those who run from all suffering
are children! I love children, but how can I love those
who want to be children all their lives? And that is how it

is with all of you, who, in your dismal infantile fear of pain and darkness, run from suffering into activity.

See what you have accomplished with all your fuss and bustle and sooty occupations! What have you got left? Your money is gone and with it all the glitter of your cowardly busyness. And what true action has all your activity engendered? Where is the great man, the shining hero, the man of action? Where is your Kaiser? Who is to take his place? And where is your art? Where are the works that would justify your times? Where are the great, joyful ideas? Ah, you have suffered far too little and not nearly well enough to produce anything good and radiant!

For true action, good and radiant action, my friends, does not spring from activity, from busy bustling, it does not spring from industrious hammering. It grows in the solitude of the mountains, it grows on the summits where silence and danger dwell. It grows out of the suffering which you have not yet learned to suffer.

ON SOLITUDE

My young friends, you ask after the school of suffering, the forge of destiny. Don't you know? No, you who are forever talking of the people and dealing with the masses, who wish to suffer only with them and for them, you do not know. I am speaking of solitude.

Solitude is the path over which destiny endeavors to lead man to himself. Solitude is the path that men most fear. A path fraught with terrors, where snakes and toads lie in wait. The men who have walked alone, those who have explored the deserts of solitude: is it not said that they went astray, that they were evil or sick? And heroic deeds: do men not speak of them as though they had been the work of criminals—because they think it best to discourage themselves from taking the path to such deeds?

And Zarathustra himself—is it not said that he died in madness and that at bottom everything he said and did was madness? And when you heard such talk, didn't you feel the blood rushing to your cheeks? As though it might have been nobler and worthier of you to become one of those madmen, as though you were ashamed of your lack of courage?

My dear friends, let me sing you the song of solitude. Without solitude there is no suffering, without solitude there is no heroism. But the solitude I have in mind is not the solitude of the blithe poets or of the theater, where the fountain bubbles so sweetly at the mouth of the hermit's cave.

From childhood to manhood is only one step, one single step. In taking that step you break away from father and mother, you become yourself; it is a step into solitude. No one takes it completely. Even the holiest hermit, the grumpiest old bear in the bleakest of mountains, takes with him, or draws after him, a thread that binds him to his father and mother, to the loving warmth of kinship and friendship. My friends, when you speak so fervently of people and fatherland, I see the thread dangling from you, and I smile. When your great men speak of their "task" and responsibility, that thread hangs out of their mouths. Your great men, your leaders and orators, never speak of tasks directed against themselves, they never speak of responsibility to destiny! They hang by a thread that leads them back to mother and to all the cozy warmth that the poets recall when they sing of childhood and its pure joys. No one severs the thread entirely, except in death and then only if he succeeds in dying his own death.

Most men, the herd, have never tasted solitude. They leave father and mother, but only to crawl to a wife and quietly succumb to new warmth and new ties. They are never alone, they never commune with themselves. And when a solitary man crosses their path, they fear him and hate him like the plague; they fling stones at him and find no peace until they are far away from him. The air around him smells of stars, of cold stellar spaces; he lacks the soft warm fragrance of the home and hatchery.

Zarathustra has something of this starry smell, this forbidding coldness. Zarathustra has gone a long way on the path of solitude. He has attended the school of suffering. He has seen the forge of destiny and been wrought in it.

Ah, my friends, I don't know whether I ought to tell you any more about solitude. I should gladly tempt you to take that path, I should gladly sing you a song of the icy raptures of cosmic space. But I know that few men can travel that path without injury. It is hard, my dear friends, to live without a mother; it is hard to live without home and people, without fatherland or fame, without the pleasures of life in a community. It is hard to live in the cold, and most of those who have started on the path have fallen. A man must be indifferent to the possibility of falling, if he wants to taste of solitude and to face up to his own destiny. It is easier and sweeter to walk with a people, with a multitude—even through misery. It is

easier and more comforting to devote oneself to the
"tasks" of the day, the tasks meted out by the collectivity.
See how happy the people are in their crowded streets!
Shots are being fired, their lives are in danger, yet every
one of them would far rather die with the masses than
walk alone in the cold outer night.

But how, my young friends, could I tempt you or lead
you? Solitude is not chosen, any more than destiny is
chosen. Solitude comes to us if we have within us the
magic stone that attracts destiny. Many, far too many,
have gone out into the desert and led the lives of herd
men in a pretty hermitage beside a lovely spring. While
others stand in the thick of the crowd, and yet the air of
the stars blows round their heads.

But blessed be he who has found his solitude, not the
solitude pictured in painting or poetry, but his own,
unique, predestined solitude. Blessed be he who knows
how to suffer! Blessed be he who bears the magic stone in
his heart. To him comes destiny, from him comes authentic action.

SPARTACUS

You have asked what I think of those who have let
themselves be named after Spartacus.

Of all those in your fatherland who are trying so hard
to usher in a better future, it is those rebellious slaves
that I still like best. How resolute they are, how direct
and straightforward! Truly, if along with their other
talents your bourgeoisie had the merest fraction of their
inner strength, your country would be saved.

But it will not be destroyed by the Spartacists. Is it not

strange, is it not destiny, that they should bear this name? They, the untaught, the raw-fisted workers, they who despise Latinists and the educated classes, have let one of their leaders paint them with a name that stinks to heaven of history and erudition! And yet, is there not a destiny in the name they have fished up from such remote times?

For there is one good thing about this new name, this so ancient name: to those who understand it, it recalls a turning point, the beginning of an end. Just as that ancient world came to an end, so must our present world: that is what the name tells us, and it is right. It must die along with all the beautiful, well-loved things that attached us to it. But was it Spartacus who destroyed the ancient world? Or was it Jesus of Nazareth, or the barbarians, or the hordes of blond mercenaries? No, Spartacus was an excellent historic hero; he shook mightily on his chains and wielded his knife bravely. But he did not transform slaves into men, and only in a secondary role did he contribute to the downfall of the ruling class of his time.

But don't look down on those men with the red fist and the schoolbook name! They are prepared, they have an intimation of destiny, they are ready to face doom. Respect the spirit that lives in those resolute men! Desperation is not heroism—you discovered that yourselves in the war. But desperation is better than the sordid fear of the bourgeoisie, who resort to heroism only when their moneybags are threatened!

What they call "communism" is well known to us; it is an old recipe, so old that it has become rather comical, from the ancient alchemist's kitchen. Pay no attention to what they say! But pay attention to what they do! Those men are capable of true action because, if only by an ignominious bypath, they have come close to the point where destiny burgeons. You have greater and nobler possibilities than they, but you are still at the beginning of the road. They are at the end, and they, my friends, are superior to you in the important sense that all those who are prepared for doom are superior to the hesitant late-comers.

THE FATHERLAND AND ITS ENEMIES

My friends, you lament too much over the downfall of your fatherland. If your fatherland must go under, it would be more dignified and more manly to let it die in silence, without whimpering! But where do you see this downfall? Or does your "fatherland" still mean nothing more to you than your moneybags and your ships? Or your Kaiser? Or the old operatic splendor?

If by fatherland you mean what the best of you once loved as the best in your people, what your nations once enriched and rejoiced the world with, then I fail to see how you can talk of downfall and doom. You have lost much, in money and provinces, in ships and world power. If that is too much for you to bear, then die by your own hands at the foot of a statue of the Kaiser, and I will sing a dirge for you. But don't stand there whimpering, en-treating history to have mercy. You, who only a short while ago were singing the song of the German spirit that was to heal the world, don't stand by the roadside now like punished schoolchildren, crying out for pity! If you cannot bear poverty, then die! If you cannot govern yourselves without a Kaiser and victorious generals, let foreigners govern you! But, I implore you, don't lose all sense of shame!

But, you protest, are our enemies not cruel? Are they not treacherous and ruthless in their victory, which was the victory of vastly superior power? Do they not talk of right and practice might? Do they not speak of justice when they mean pillage and rapine?

You are right. I am not defending your enemies. I have no love for them. They too, like yourselves, are base in victory, full of tricks and subterfuges. —But, friends, has it ever been otherwise? And is it our mission to keep up these loud lamentations over what cannot be helped?

Our mission, it seems to me, is to die like men or to go on living like men. Not to bawl like babies, but to recognize our destiny, to embrace our suffering, to transform its bitterness into sweetness, to mature through our suffering. Our goal cannot be to grow great and rich and powerful again, to have ships and armies again as quickly as possible. Our goal cannot be a childish delusion— haven't we seen what comes of ships and armies, of power and money? Have we already forgotten?

Young men of Germany, our goal cannot be marked off by names and figures. Our goal, like the goal of every human being, is to become one with our destiny. If we can do that, it makes no difference whether we are great or small, rich or poor, feared or ridiculed. Let the soldiers' councils and the workers of the pen make speeches about such things! If you have not come to yourselves through war and suffering, if you are still determined to change destiny and run away from suffering, if you refuse to grow up, then perish!

But you understand me, I can see it in your eyes. You sniff out consolation in the bitter words of the Old Man of the Mountain, the Wicked Old Man. You remember words he has said to you about suffering, about destiny, about solitude. Don't you feel a breath of solitude in the suffering that has befallen you? Hasn't your hearing become sharpened to the still voice of destiny? Don't you feel that your pain can bear fruit? That your suffering can become a privilege, a call to the highest things?

Just this I ask of you: don't set yourselves aims at a time when the infinite lies before you! Don't harness yourself to purposes now that destiny has shattered all your fine purposes of yesterday! God has spoken to you; I beg you, don't be ashamed of it! Look upon yourselves as elected, as called, as chosen! But not chosen for this or that, for world power or commerce, democracy or socialism! You are chosen to become yourselves in suffering, to recapture in pain your own breath and heartbeat, which you had lost. You are chosen to breathe the air of the stars and from children to become men.

Cease to lament, my young friends! Cease to weep the tears of childhood because you have parted from your mother and her sweet bread. Learn to eat bitter bread, men's bread, the bread of destiny!

Then the "fatherland" which the best of your ancestors envisioned and loved will reappear to you. Then you will return from your solitude to a community that is no longer a stable and hatchery, to a community of men, a realm without frontiers, the kingdom of God as your fathers called it. There you will find room for every virtue, even if your national boundaries are narrow. There you will find room for every kind of courage, even without generals!

Children that you are, Zarathustra cannot withhold his laughter at having to comfort you like this!

WORLD BETTERMENT

Young friends, there is an expression that dismays me when I hear it in your mouths—when it does not make me laugh! That expression is "world betterment." You used to sing that song in your associations and herds; your Kaiser and all your prophets were especially given to that song: the German soul, went the refrain, will make the world whole.

Friends, we must learn to desist from judging whether the world is good or bad, and we must forgo the strange pretension that it is up to us to better it.

The world has often been denounced as bad, because the denouncer had slept badly or had too much to eat. The world has often been praised as a paradise, because the praiser had just kissed a girl.

The world wasn't made to be bettered. Nor were you made to be bettered. You were made to be yourselves. You were made to enrich the world with a sound, a tone, a shadow. Be yourself, then the world will be rich and beautiful! Be other than yourself, be a liar and a coward, then the world will be poor and seem in need of betterment.

Now in particular, in these strange times, the song of world betterment is being sung again with a will, shouted from the rooftops. Can't you hear how ugly and drunken it sounds? How insensitive, how unhappy, how unintelligent and unwise? And this song is like a frame that can be fitted to any picture. It fitted the Kaiser and his policemen; it fitted your famous German professors, Zarathustra's old friends! This ungainly song fits democracy and socialism, the League of Nations and world peace; it fits the abolition of nationalism, and the new nationalism as well. Your enemies are singing it too; you are like two choruses trying to sing each other into the ground. Haven't you noticed that wherever this song is struck up men reach for their pockets; it is a song of self-interest and self-seeking—alas, not the noble self-seeking that elevates and steels the self, but the self-seeking that hinges on money and moneybags, vanities and delusions. When man becomes ashamed of his self-seeking, he speaks of world betterment; he hides behind such words.

I don't know, my friends, whether the world has ever been bettered. Perhaps it has always been as good and as bad as it is. I don't know, I am not a philosopher, I have too little curiosity in that direction. But this I do know: if the world has ever been bettered, if it has ever been made richer, more alive, happier, more dangerous, more amusing, this has not been the work of reformers, of betterers, but of true self-seekers, among whom I should so like to count you. Those earnestly and truly self-seeking men who have no goal and no purposes, who are content to live and to be themselves. They suffer much, but they suffer willingly. They are willing to be sick, provided they are privileged to die their own death, the death that they themselves have come by, their very own!

By such men the world has perhaps been bettered now and then—just as an autumn day is made better by a little cloud, a little brown shadow, a swift flight of birds. There is no reason to believe that the world needs more betterment than it can obtain from the presence of a few men—not cattle, not a herd, but a few men, a few of the rare beings who rejoice us as a flight of birds or a tree by the seashore rejoices us—by the mere fact that they exist, that there are such men. If you are ambitious, my young friends, if you want to strive after honor, then strive after this honor! But such striving is dangerous, it leads through solitude, and it can easily cost you your lives.

ON THE GERMANS

Have you never wondered how it happens that the Germans have been so little loved, that they have been so profoundly hated, so greatly feared and so passionately shunned? Has it not seemed strange to you that in this last war, which you entered into with so many soldiers and such excellent prospects, one nation after another, slowly but surely, went over to your enemies, forsook you and put you in the wrong?

Yes, you noticed, you noticed it with profound indignation, and you were proud to be so forsaken, alone, and misunderstood. —But hear me, you were not misunderstood! It was you yourselves who did not understand, who were mistaken.

You young Germans have always prided yourselves on the very virtues you did not possess, and blamed your enemies most for the vices they had learned from you. You have always spoken of "German" virtues; you held that loyalty and the kindred virtues had as good as been invented by your Kaiser or your people. But you yourselves were not loyal; you were untrue to yourselves, and that alone is what won you the hatred of the world. You say: no, it was our money, it was our success! And perhaps your enemies thought so too, perhaps they concurred in your shopkeeper's logic. But the true causes are always a little deeper than people think, and especially than the snap judgments of unimaginative businessmen. Perhaps your enemies did begrudge you your money, perhaps it aroused their envy! But there are also kinds of success which arouse no envy, which the world greets with rejoicing. Why did you never have such success, why always the other kind?

Because you were untrue to yourselves. You played a role that was not yours. With the help of your Kaiser and of Richard Wagner, you made the "German virtues" into an opera which no one in the world took seriously but yourselves. And behind all the operatic flimflam you let your dark, slavish, megalomaniacal instincts run rampant. You always had the name of God on your lips and your hand on your purse. You spoke of order, virtue, organization, and meant moneymaking. And you gave yourselves away by always attributing the same sort of skulduggery to the enemy. Hear, you said, hear how they talk of virtue and justice, and see what they do in reality. You winked at one another when an Englishman or American made fine speeches, because you knew what is behind such speeches. But how did you know if not by your own hearts?

Very well. Tell me I'm hurting you! You're not accustomed to being hurt, you're accustomed to patting each other on the back. You had the enemy to revile, to discharge your aggressions on; you were always right, the enemy was always wrong. But I say to you: you must be able to inflict pain and suffer it, if you want to side with life and make your own way in the world. The world is a cold place; it is not a home and hatchery where you can sit in eternal childhood and sheltered warmth. The world is cruel and incalculable; it loves only the strong and the able, it loves those who remain true to themselves. Others can achieve only short-lived success—the kind of success that you, since the spiritual downfall of Germany, had achieved with your commodities and organizations! What has become of that success? But now perhaps your time has come. Perhaps the need is great enough to tense your will—not to more fuss and bustle, not to another flight from the secret meaning of life, but to new manhood, faith in yourselves, truth and loyalty to yourselves.

Because, my friends, with all my angry scolding, this must have come through to you: that I love you, that I have a certain confidence in you, that I sense a future in you—and believe me, old hermit and weather maker that I am, I have a keen and many-times-tested sense of smell. Yes, I believe in you—there is something in you, in the German people, that I believe in and have always deeply loved. It is something that cannot yet be seen—possibilities, a future, an alluring Perhaps, flashing behind a hundred clouds. I believe in it precisely because you are still children, because you do so many childish things, because you carry your long, so very long childhood about with you. Ah, if only this childhood should one day grow to manhood! If only this credulity should one day become confidence, this tenderness goodness, this eccentricity and sensibility character and virile self-will!

You are the most pious people in the world. But what gods your piety has created! Kaisers and drill sergeants! And now, in their stead, these new bringers of good tidings to the world!

May you learn to seek the God within yourselves! May

you one day stand as much in awe of this secret something, this future in yourselves, as you did formerly of
princes and banners! May your piety one day cease to
kneel and stand upright on strong, manly, well-hardened
legs!

YOU AND YOUR PEOPLE

You are still distrustful, my friends; you often look at
me askance, and I know what displeases you and disturbs
you in me: you are afraid that Zarathustra, the Pied
Piper, will lure you away from the people you love, the
people you hold sacred! Isn't that so? Haven't I guessed
right?

Your teachers and books teach two doctrines: the one is
that the people or nation is everything; the second
reverses the first.

But Zarathustra has never been a teacher; to him your
doctrines are laughable at best. Dear friends, the choice
whether to be a nation or individuals is not open to you.
No man ever attained the summits of solitude or manhood by reading about them in a book and deciding to
head in that direction.

But if, my young friends, I ask you: What does your
people so yearn for? What is its need?—you will say: Our
people needs actions, our people needs men who do not
merely talk but know how to act!

So be it, my friends, but whether for your own sake or
for the sake of your people, remember what gives rise to
actions, what gives rise to the cold, joyful, manly self-will,
to the spirit of morning from which actions spring as
lightning from a cloud. Have you forgotten so soon?
Don't you recall?

Friends, what your people and every people need is men who have learned to be themselves, who have recognized their destiny. They alone become the destiny of their people. They alone refuse to be satisfied with speeches and decrees and a bureaucracy without courage or sense of responsibility. They alone have the courage, the vitality, the healthy, joyful, well-wrought good humor that gives rise to true actions.

You Germans more than any other people are accustomed to obedience. Your people has obeyed so easily, so very willingly and gladly, reluctant to take the slightest step that did not afford the satisfaction of carrying out an order, of complying with a regulation. Signposts telling you what to do, and above all what not to do, covered your country like a forest. How obedient such a people will surely be if, after so long a pause, so long a period of weary waiting, it should once again hear the voices of men! If instead of decrees and regulations it should once again hear a tone of inner strength and conviction? If once again it should see actions, not most condescendingly commanded and most humbly carried out, but springing bright and full-blown from their father's head like the Greek goddess?

Bear that always in mind, my friends, and never forget what it is that a people hungers and thirsts for! Never forget that action and manhood are not to be found in books or public speeches. They are found on mountain-tops, and the road to them leads through suffering and solitude, through suffering borne gladly, and voluntary solitude.

And unlike all your public speakers, I call out to you: There is no great hurry! From all sides they cry: "Run! Hurry! Decide this minute! The world is on fire! The fatherland is in danger!" But believe me: the fatherland will suffer no harm if you take your time, if you let your will, your destiny, your action ripen! Haste, like ready obedience, is one of those German virtues that are not virtues.

Children, don't hang your heads so! Don't make old Zarathustra laugh!

Is it a calamity to have been born into fresh, stormy, blustering times? Isn't it your good fortune?

THE LEAVETAKING

And now, my friends, I take leave of you. And you know that when Zarathustra takes leave of his listeners, he does not ask them to remain true to him, to be good disciples.

You must not worship Zarathustra. You must not try to become Zarathustra. In each one of you there is a hidden being, still in the deep sleep of childhood. Bring it to life! In each one of you there is a call, a will, an impulse of nature, an impulse toward the future, the new, the higher. Let it mature, let it resound, nurture it! Your future is not this or that; it is not money or power, it is not wisdom or success at your trade—your future, your hard dangerous path is this: to mature and to find God in yourselves. Nothing, O young men of Germany, has been made harder for you. You have always looked for God, but never in yourselves. He is nowhere else. There is no other God than the God within you.

If I should come again, my friends, we shall talk of other things, of happier, more pleasant things. Then, I hope, we shall sit together and walk together like men, side by side but each of us strong and himself, relying on nothing else in the world than himself and the fortune that favors the strong and the daring.

Go now, go back to your streets with all their speakers. Forget what the stranger from the mountains has said to you. Zarathustra has never been a guide. He has always been a joker and a moody wanderer.

Don't let any speaker or teacher, whoever he may be, put a bee in your bonnet. In each of you there is only one bee, his very own, that he has any need to listen to.

This I say to you in parting: Listen to that bee, listen to the voice that comes from within yourself! When that voice falls silent, know that something is amiss, that something is out of joint, that you are on the wrong road.

But if your bee speaks—then heed it, follow its every lure, even into the remotest and coldest solitude, even into the darkest destiny!

Letter to a Young German
1919

YOU WRITE ME that you are in despair and do not know what to believe, what to hope. You do not know whether or not there is a God. You do not know whether or not life has any meaning, whether or not love of country has a meaning, whether, in the wretched condition of the world, it is better to strive for spiritual goods or merely to fill your belly.

I believe your state of mind and soul to be the right one. Not to know whether there is a God, not to know whether there is good and evil, is far better than to know for sure. Five years ago, if you remember, I should say you were pretty well convinced there was a God, and above all you had no doubt as to what was good and what was evil. Naturally you did what you thought was good and marched off to war. For five years now, the best years of your youth, you have kept on doing "good": you have fired a gun, gone over the top, lounged about in barracks and mud holes, buried comrades or bandaged their wounds. And little by little you began to doubt the good, to suspect that the good and glorious occupation you were engaged in was fundamentally evil, or at the very least stupid and absurd.

And so it was. Evidently the good you were so sure of at the time was not the right good, the good that is inde-

structible and timeless; and evidently the God you knew
in those days was not the right God. Presumably he was
the national God of our consistories and war poets, the
awesome God whose props and footstool are cannon and
whose favorite colors are black, white, and red. A God he
assuredly was, a mighty, gigantic God, greater than any
Jehovah; hundreds of thousands of bloody battle sacrifices were offered up to him, and in his honor hundreds of
thousands of bellies were slit open, hundreds of thousands of lungs torn to pieces; he was more bloodthirsty
and brutal than any idol, and during the bloody sacrifice
the priests at home, our theologians, intoned their well-
paid paeans of praise to him. The last vestige of religion
we possessed in our impoverished souls and so impoverished, soul-less churches was lost. Has anyone stopped to
consider, and to wonder at the fact, that in those four
years of war our theologians buried their own religion,
their own Christianity? Committed to the service of love,
they preached hatred; committed to the service of mankind, they mistook for mankind the authorities who paid
them. They proved (not all of course, but the spokes-
men) with guile and many words that war and Christianity were perfectly compatible, that a man could be the
best of Christians and yet shoot and stab to perfection.
But that is not true, and if our national Churches had not
been national Churches in the service of Throne and
Army, but Churches of God, they would have given us
during the war what we so bitterly lacked: a haven of
humanity, a sanctuary for the orphaned soul, a perpetual
admonition to moderation, wisdom, and brotherly love; in
short, they would have offered divine services.

I beg you not to misunderstand me! I blame no one. I

am only trying to tell you what was, not to accuse. This is unusual in our country; all we hear is cries of accusation and hatred. Today we Germans like everyone else have learned the disastrous art of putting the blame on others when we are in trouble. I am attacking, accusing, this attitude and nothing else. We are all of us equally guilty and innocent of the fact that our faith was so weak and our officially patented God so ruthless, that we were so incapable of distinguishing war and peace, good and evil. You and I, the Kaiser and the priest, all played a part; we have no call to accuse one another.

If you are now wondering where to look for consolation, where to seek a new and better God, a new and better faith, you will surely realize, in your present loneliness and despair, that this time you must not look to external, official sources, to Bibles, pulpits, or thrones, for enlightenment. Nor to me. You can find it only in yourself. And there it is, there dwells the God who is higher and more selfless than the patriots' God of 1914. The sages of all time have proclaimed him, but he does not come to us from books, he lives within us, and all our knowledge of him is worthless unless he opens our inner eye. This God is in you too. He is most particularly in you, the dejected and despairing. It is not the inferior man who sickens with the affliction of the times, or who becomes dissatisfied with the gods and idols of the past.

But search where you may, no prophet or teacher can relieve you of the need to look within. Today the entire German people, all of us, are in your situation. Our world has collapsed, our pride has been humbled, our money is gone, our friends are dead. And now, persisting in our deplorable old habit, we are all—or nearly all—looking for the villain who was to blame for it all. We call him America, we call him Clemenceau, we call him Kaiser Wilhelm or heaven knows what else, and with all our accusations we are running around in a circle that gets us nowhere. It is childish and stupid to ask whether this one or that one is guilty. I propose that for one short hour we ask ourselves instead: "What about myself? What has been my share of the guilt? When have I been too loud-mouthed, too arrogant, too credulous, too boastful? What is there in me that may have helped to foster the rabble-rousing press, the degenerate religion of the national Jehovah, and all the illusions that have so suddenly collapsed?"

The hour in which we raise questions is not a pleasant one. We see that we are weak, small, and corrupt; we are humbled. But not crushed. Because we also see that in all this there is no guilt. Neither the wicked Kaiser nor the wicked Clemenceau is to blame; neither the victorious democratic nations nor the vanquished barbarians are right. Guilt and innocence are childish simplifications, and to recognize this is our first step into the temple of a new God. It will not show us how to prevent future wars or how to become rich. But we shall have learned one thing: to stop submitting the crucial problems of our life, our questions of "guilt" and conscience, to an old-style Jehovah, a top sergeant or a newspaper editor, but to solve them in our own hearts. We must resolve to grow up, to become men. Looking back on the loss of our fleet, our machines, and our money, posterity may take this view: a child's pretty toys were taken away; then, after weeping and wailing for a time, the child pulled himself together and became a man. That is what we must do, there is no other way. And each one of us must take the first step by himself, in his own heart.

Since you are devoted to Nietzsche, reread the last pages of the "untimely meditation" on the advantages and disadvantages of studying history. Read word for word the passage about the younger generation fated to demolish a crumbling pseudo-culture and to begin anew! How hard, how bitter is the lot of such a generation, and how great, how holy! You are such a younger generation—you young people of today in this defeated Germany! Upon your shoulders lies this burden, upon your hearts this task.

But don't confine yourself to Nietzsche, or to any other prophet or guide. Our mission is not to instruct you, to make things easier for you, to show you the way. Our mission is solely to remind you that there is a God and only one God; he dwells in your hearts, and it is there that you must seek him out and speak with him.

Thou Shalt Not Kill

1919

THE TAMING OF MAN, his development from gorilla to civilized being, is a long, slow process. The advances thus far embodied in law and custom are fragile; time and again what seemed to be definitive achievements are negated by an atavistic gnashing of teeth. If we see our provisional goal in the fulfillment of the spiritual imperatives put forth by the spiritual leaders of mankind from Zoroaster and Lao-tzu down, we are compelled to say that present-day mankind is still far closer to the gorilla than to man. We are not yet human, we are on the way to humanity.

A few thousand years ago the religious law of a superior people handed down the fundamental maxim: "Thou shalt not kill." In the spring of 1919 Baron Wrangel, addressing a small international gathering of idealists in Bern, put forward the demand that in future no man must be compelled to kill another man—"not even in the service of his country." And this was felt to be a significant step forward. That is how far we have come. Some thousands of years after Moses formulated the commandment on Mount Sinai, it is restated very cautiously and with restrictions by a small group of well-intended men. Not a single civilized people has embodied it without restriction in its legal code. Everywhere men are still timidly discussing this simplest and soundest of all imperatives. Every student of Lao-tzu, every disciple of Jesus, every follower of Francis of Assisi was centuries in advance of the law and reason of the present-day civilized world.

This would seem to argue against the value of such lofty demands and to demonstrate purely and simply that man is incapable of progress. A hundred other examples might be cited in support of the same contention. Actually, our dismal experience does not detract from the value of such humanitarian imperatives and insights. For thousands of years the maxim "Thou shalt not kill" has been honored and faithfully followed. After the Old Testament came a New Testament; Christ was possible, the partial emancipation of the Jews was possible, mankind produced Goethe, Mozart, and Dostoevsky. At all times there has been a minority of men of good will, who believed in the future and obeyed laws that are inscribed in no secular legal code. And during this horrible war, thousands of men acted in accordance with unwritten higher laws; soldiers treated enemies with mercy and respect, while others suffered imprisonment and torture because they staunchly rejected the duty of murdering and hating.

In order to esteem such men and deeds at their full worth, in order to overcome our doubt in the progress of man from animal to human being, we must live in faith. We must learn to value ideas as highly as bullets or gold pieces, to love possibilities and cultivate them in ourselves; we must gain intimations of the future and of the future in our own hearts.

The "practical" man, who is always right in committee meetings, is invariably wrong outside of his committees.

Ideals and faith in the future are always right. They are the one source from which the world draws strength. And anyone who disposes of humanitarian ideas as idle talk and fuzzy thinking or of strivings for the future as literature is still a gorilla and has a long way to go before becoming a man.

A good example that even our "practical" men will appreciate: In his colonial reminiscences Carl Peters relates how he once ordered some African natives to plant coconut palms. The natives refused to do anything so fatiguing and pointless. Peters explained to them that in eight or ten years the trees planted today would be full-grown and reward their pains a hundredfold. Of that the natives were well aware, they were far from stupid. But it struck them as sheer madness that a man should work his fingers to the bone for a reward that would be forthcoming only in ten years. White men had such comical ideas!

It is we men of the spirit, we poets, seers, fools, and dreamers, who plant trees for later. Many of our trees will not thrive, many of our seeds will be sterile, many of our dreams will turn out to be mistakes, delusions, and false hopes. Where is the harm in that?

But there is no point in trying to make practical men out of poets, calculators out of believers, organizers out of dreamers. During the war, artists, writers, and intellectuals were transformed into soldiers and farm workers. Now efforts are being made to "politicize" them and turn them into organs of material change. That is like trying to drive a nail with a barometer. Because today the times are hard, it is thought that all energies should be directed to our daily needs, every will harnessed to the practical work of the hour.

But though the need cries out to high heaven, fuss and

bustle are useless. The world will not progress any faster if you turn poets into street speakers and philosophers into cabinet ministers. It will progress wherever men do what they were made for, what their nature demands of them, what they consequently do willingly and well. And even if practical men regard such things as luxuries, concern for the future, faith in man as he will be some day, and groping play with remote possibilities will always be every bit as important as political organization, the building of houses, and the baking of bread.

And we believers in the future will never cease to concern ourselves with the old commandment: "Thou shalt not kill." Even if some day all the legal codes in the world forbid killing (inclusive of killing in war and killing by executioners), that imperative will never lose its cogency, It is the foundation of all progress, all human development. We kill so much! Not only in our stupid battles, the stupid street fighting of our revolution, our stupid executions—no, we kill at every step. We kill when circumstances force us to drive gifted young people into occupations for which they are not suited. We kill when we close our eyes to poverty, affliction, or infamy. We kill when, because it is easier, we countenance or even pretend to approve of atrophied social, political, educational, and religious institutions, instead of resolutely combating them. Just as a consistent socialist looks on property as theft, so those who hold consistently to our kind of faith regard all contempt for human life, all cruelty and indifference, as tantamount to killing. And not only things present can be killed, but the things of the future as well. A great deal of future in a young man can be killed by a little mordant skepticism. Everywhere life is waiting, everywhere the future holds promise, and we see so little, we trample so much. We kill at every step.

In respect to mankind we all of us have but one task. To help mankind as a whole make some small advance, to better a particular institution, to do away with one particular mode of killing—all these are commendable, but they are not my task and yours. Our task as men is this: in our own unique personal lives, to take a short step on the road from animal to man.

Thoughts about China

1921

THE EYES OF THE WORLD are fixed in eager expectation upon a congress now being held in Washington
for the purpose of preventing a war between the United
States and Japan and limiting the naval armament of the
great powers. Its work has been partially successful;
something has been accomplished. There will not be a
war between Japan and the United States in the fore-
seeable future, and less money and labor will be squan-
dered on battleships.

The world has been less attentive to another aspect of
the discussions in Washington. The great and powerful
nations have achieved a certain measure of agreement.
But little heed was given to a weak nation that was also
present. I am speaking of China. The oldest world power
in existence, vast and ancient China, has not chosen the
path of adaptation to the Western world that Japan has
been following consistently for several decades. China
has become very weak; it has virtually ceased to be an
independent power and is looked upon by the great
powers as little more than a "sphere of influence" to be
cautiously divided among them.

Years ago a Chinese devotee of his country's old and
venerable ideas spoke of these developments in terms that
have no bearing on politics but are close to the spirit of

the Tao Tê Ching. He spoke roughly as follows: Let the Japanese or other nations conquer us, take possession of our country, and run our government. Let them! It will be seen that we are the weaker, that we can be conquered and gobbled up. Let that happen, if that is China's destiny! But when the others have gobbled us up, it remains to be seen whether they will be able to digest us. It may well turn out that our government and army, administration and finances will be Japanese, American, and English but that the conquerors will be powerless to change China, that on the contrary they will be conquered and changed by the spirit of China. For China is weak in the art of war and in political organization but rich in life, rich in spirit, rich in ancient culture.

I remembered that amiable Chinese when I read the latest reports from Washington. And I thought: even now, while China though not yet conquered is consummating its decline as a world power, it has conquered a large part of the West! In the last twenty years the ancient Chinese culture, previously known only to the merest handful of scholars, has begun to conquer us through translations of its ancient books, through the influence of its ancient thinking. In the last ten years Lao-tzu has become known through translations into any number of languages and achieved enormous influence throughout Europe. Formerly, until twenty years ago, when we spoke of the "culture of the East," we thought exclusively of India, of the Vedas, Buddha, and the Bhagavad-Gita. Now, when we speak of East Asian culture, we think equally or perhaps still more of China, of Chinese art, of Lao-tzu, of Chuang-tzu, or Li Po. And it turns out that for us Europeans the thinking of ancient

China, especially that of early Taoism, far from being a mere exotic curiosity, provides significant corroboration of our own thinking, and invaluable counsel and help. Not that from these ancient books of wisdom we can suddenly gain a new and redeeming view of life; not that we ought to cast away our Western culture and become Chinese! But in the ancient Chinese, and especially in Lao-tzu, we find reminders of a mode of thought that we have neglected, a recognition and cultivation of energies that we, busy with other things, have too long disregarded.

I go to the Chinese corner of my library—a peaceful, happy corner! What wisdom there is in these ancient books and how amazingly timely it can be! How often during the terrible war years they yielded up thoughts that consoled and revived my spirits!

Picking up a notebook in which I have jotted down quotations, I read a message from Yang Chu.

A man's attitude toward life, says this Chinese philosopher, possibly a contemporary of Lao-tzu and earlier than Buddha, should be that of a master toward his servant. Then follows the Maxim of the Four Dependencies:

"Most men are dependent on four things which they desire too greatly: long life; fame; title and rank; money and possessions.

"It is their unremitting desire for these four things that makes men fear demons and fear one another, that makes them fear the mighty and fear punishment. Every state is built upon this fourfold fear and dependency.

"Men who are prey to these four dependencies live like madmen. They may be slain or they may be permitted to live; in either case destiny comes to these men from without.

"That man, however, who loves his destiny and knows himself to be one with it—cares nothing for long life, for fame, for rank or wealth!

"Such men carry peace within them. Nothing in the world can threaten them, nothing can be hostile to them. They bear their destiny within their own selves!"

World Crisis and Books
ANSWER TO A QUESTIONNAIRE
1937

O F COURSE there are any number of good and beautiful books that I should like to see widely read.
But books that might be expected to make for a better
world and a more smiling future there are none. I fear
that our present crisis, though not the end of our civilization, will look very much like it; along with so many other
beautiful things that we love, many books will vanish
forever. Ideas which yesterday were held sacred,which a
small number of spiritual men still prize and try to live
by, may tomorrow be utterly discredited and forgotten—
all but an indestructible core which must serve as the
leaven for any renewal. As long as there are men, that
core will never be lost, it is man's one "eternal" possession.

This supreme possession of mankind has left its deposit
in many forms and languages: the Bible and the sacred
books of ancient China, the Indian Vedanta and various
other books and collections of books are the embodiments
of what little man has truly known down to our day.
These embodiments are not without ambiguity; these
books are not eternal, but they contain the spiritual heritage of our history. All other literature has radiated from
them and would not exist without them: all Christian
literature, for example, down to Dante and our own day,

is an emanation of the New Testament, and if this entire
literature were lost but the New Testament preserved,
similar literatures might well spring from it at any time.
Only the few "sacred books" of mankind have this genera-
tive power; they alone outlive all the millennia and crises.
One comforting thought is that their dissemination is not
important. It need not be millions who inwardly take possession of, or rather are possessed by, this or that sacred
book: a few suffice.

Page from a Notebook
1940

JULIAN GREEN writes in his journal that he has no talent whatsoever for atheism; it seems to him that he has never in all his life doubted the existence of God. Of all the self-revealing statements made in this extraordinarily rich journal, this, I believe, is the most important.

There are readers of Julian Green who are irritated by his profession of absolute belief in God and hold that his novels contradict it. These readers find the novels beautiful in some mysterious way, or at least interesting, but on the whole they regard them as "negative," that is, destructive, defeatist, skeptical, and sick, because the author often seems to tear reality to shreds and to doubt just about everything, not only conventions but the reality of phenomena in general.

I see no contradiction. On the contrary, Green's belief in God and disbelief in the world are mutually complementary. Green believes in God; for him God is substance, reality as such. The world in which the believer lives, the material everyday world around him, is what separates him from God. It shuts him off from God as a room or a house shuts us off from the air and the sky. That is why nothing in this world interests him, fascinates him so much as the chinks, the flaws, he finds in reality.

He rushes to these chinks, for through them the eye has access to God. When we see Green digging into the chinks and flaws of the world, what fascinates him is not so much the chinks, the defects, the rot, as what lies behind them: God.

FROM A LETTER

I am sending you the final draft of a new poem. Except for purely mechanical daily chores, I have done nothing in the past few weeks but tinker with this poem. It has gone through eight or nine intermediate stages and now I am going to let it stand. A funny thing: with half the world getting ready, in trenches and bunkers, in shipyards and factories, to reduce our world to dust and splinters, I have spent all these days trying to improve my little poem.

Let me tell you about it: First the poem had four stanzas; now it has only three. I hope this has made it simpler and better and that nothing has been lost. The fourth line of the first stanza bothered me from the start, it was obviously makeshift. I copied the poem several times for friends and each time I was more dissatisfied, each time the line seemed more inept and fatal to the poem, more like a filler. And finally, among the friends who read the poem, there was one with particularly sensitive ears who didn't like it either; he wrote me as much, and I had to agree with him. Then I began in earnest to examine the poem line by line and word by word to find out what was superfluous and what was not.

One might ask: What is the good of such labor? Nine-tenths of my readers, no, a lot more than nine-tenths, won't even notice the difference between one version and another, though now and then one of them is amazingly right in his reactions. I haven't forgotten, though it happened thirty years ago, how a reader once asked me for the text of a short poem. He had read it in a magazine, he didn't remember which, and still knew the eight-line poem by heart—all but one line, which had slipped his mind. I looked at the manuscript; the forgotten line was the weakest, and a question mark in the margin showed me that I had queried it at the time of writing.

Be that as it may, the majority of my readers will not appreciate the pains I take in revising, or even notice it. Regardless of whether the poem is good or bad, the magazine that publishes it will pay me the usual few francs, a sum roughly equivalent to the day's wages of a skilled worker. In the eyes of the world my endeavor to improve this poem will therefore be an absurdity, a ludicrous, rather insane game. Why, it will be asked, does a poet spend so much time and effort over a few verses?

One might answer the question as follows: Of course the poet's pains may be wasted, for how likely is it that he has written one of those very few poems which survive their author and his times? Still, this man, who has no claim to be taken very seriously, has done something better, more desirable, and less harmful than most people are doing today. True, the childish fellow has manipulated words and written a poem, but he has neither fired a gun nor set off a bomb nor let loose poison gas nor manufactured munitions nor sunk ships.

And another answer might be: In selecting words and putting them down in a world that may be destroyed tomorrow, a poet is doing the same thing as the anemones and primroses and other flowers that spring up in our meadows. Perhaps the meadow will be shattered by shell-fire tomorrow or stifled by poison gas, or soldiers will dig trenches or string barbed wire across it. But the flowers do not let such possibilities—which for many of our meadows are more like probabilities—deter them. They painstakingly put forth leaves and shape their calyxes in the proper way with four or five smooth or jagged petals, as precisely as ever they can. That might be an answer. But, except for the poet himself, no one asks the question.

End of the Rigi-Journal
August 1945

N OW AND THEN the mail brings a precious surprise. Yesterday there was one: a packet of letters from Germany! Someone from Stuttgart had come to Switzerland and brought letters for me from some Swabian friends. He had sent them on to me and offered to take my answers back with him. They were no random letters from strangers but eagerly awaited communications from friends. They contained nothing new about the matters that worried me most in Germany, but in them for the first time a group of outstanding German intellectuals spoke to me of their experiences and thoughts since the collapse. None of these friends, it goes without saying, had been a supporter or beneficiary of National Socialism; they had been alert to the danger from the very first and witnessed the growth of Hitler's power with profound alarm. Many of them had proved themselves in suffering and made great sacrifices; they had lost their positions and livelihood and suffered imprisonment. For many years they had looked on, clear-sighted but helpless, as the evil mounted and the devilry became more and more monstrous. From the onset of the war they had hoped with bleeding hearts for the defeat of their own people and often wished for death. The story of this section of the German population has not yet been written;

few persons outside Germany even acknowledge its existence. Some of my correspondents were formerly Liberals
or South German Democrats, others were Catholics, a
good many were Socialists.

These intellectuals, whose suffering, I believe, has
made them the maturest and wisest people in Europe
today, endeavored, some consciously and deliberately,
some unconsciously and instinctively, to dissociate themselves from everything connected with National Socialism. In their unspeakable misery the embattled French or
Italians, the hungry and suffering Dutchmen or Greeks,
the sorely tried Poles, even the Jews who saw their fellows tortured and murdered by the hundreds of thousands—all these peoples had one advantage: solidarity,
community of fate, comradeship, allegiance to their nation. This was denied the opponents and victims of Hitler
inside Germany, except for those who were organized before 1933, and nearly all of those were killed or swal-
lowed up by the hell of the prisons and concentration
camps. There remained only an unorganized minority of
reasonable, well-intentioned men. These were harried
more and more by stool-pigeons and informers; they lived
in an atmosphere poisoned by lies, surrounded by a
people infected with a malignant and to them incompre-
hensible frenzy. I believe that most of those who have
survived the nightmare of those twelve years are broken
and no longer capable of active participation in the
reconstruction of Germany. But I also believe that they
can make an enormous contribution to the spiritual and
moral awakening of their people, who thus far have not
even begun to open their minds to what has happened
or to their own share of responsibility. In striking contrast

to the apathetic weariness of the people at large, the conscience of these men who never lost their awareness has
developed the keen sensibility of an open wound; such
men are prepared to tackle the question of national
guilt.

All the communications of these truly good Germans
have one thing in common: a sharp reaction to the tone
of the moralizing sermons that are now, rather belatedly,
being addressed by the democratic peoples to the Germans. In effectively abridged form, some of these articles
and pamphlets, among them C. G. Jung's essay "Collective Guilt," are being distributed in Germany by the
occupying powers. The only section of the German
people that is willing to read such statements today has
reacted with a terrifying touchiness. Undoubtedly the
sermons are often perfectly right; unfortunately they do
not reach the German people but only the best and
noblest section of it, whose conscience has long been only
too wide awake.

I cannot defend to my Swabian friends these articles
that I call sermons. I shall not attempt to. Altogether I
have nothing to say to these friends. What can a man who
lives in an unbombed house and eats every day, who has
had his share of trouble and worry in the last ten years
but has not even been threatened with violence, say to
people who have been through every kind of suffering?
Still, there is one point on which I feel able to advise my
friends across the border. They may be far superior to me
in everything else, but in one matter my experience goes
back farther than theirs. I broke with nationalism, all
nationalism, many years ago, not under Hitler and not
under the impact of Allied air raids, but from 1914 to

1918, and since then I have repeatedly verified and rein-
forced my opposition to nationalism. Consequently I shall
be able to write this to my friends in Swabia: "The one
thing in your letters that I do not wholly understand is
your indignation over certain articles attempting to en-
lighten your people as to their guilt. It makes me want to
cry out to you: Don't forfeit the little good that the collapse offers you! In 1918 you obtained a republic in place
of an autocratic monarchy. And today, in the midst of the
general misery, you have another opportunity, an opportunity to participate in a new episode of man's progress
toward humanity. In this you have an advantage over the
victors and neutrals: you see through the madness of all
nationalism; deep in your hearts you have long hated it,
you are in a position to free yourselves from it. You have
already done so to a considerable extent, but not radically
enough. For when you have completed this process in
yourselves, you will have entirely different things to say
about the German people and collective guilt; you will be
able to read or listen to any statement insulting or pro-
voking a whole nation without feeling that you too have
been insulted or provoked. And you, you few, will be
superior in human worth to your own people and to every
other people; you will be a step closer to the Tao."

Speech after Midnight
1946

Dear Friends:

A NEW YEAR has begun for us with its unknown promises and perils, and even if this midnight hour means no more than any other hour in our lives, we celebrate it as a festive occasion, a very solemn one, and in this we do well, for in our restless, impoverished lives every occasion to withdraw, however briefly, from everyday life and to reflect, to meditate on the past and future, to draw up a balance sheet, to examine the world and ourselves, is a blessing. Merely to reflect, whether in grief or in brave joy, on the passage of time, on the transience of our lives and undertakings, is a kind of purification and a test as well. It is as though we held up a tuning fork to the confusion of our days; its implacable clear note shows us how far we have inwardly deviated from what we should be, from our proper place in the harmony of the world. It is a good thing to strike this tuning fork now and then. It is good even when it shames us and wounds our pride.

This welcome, still untarnished New Year, it seems to me, holds a very special and important meaning. After years of slaughter and destruction, this is our first New Year's Eve without war, the first New Year's Eve in which our world is not full of torment and death, on which we no longer hear the great machines of destruction high over us in the darkness, bound on their sinister missions. True, we hardly dare utter the word "peace"; true, we still distrust the unaccustomed silence in the air; but our distrust, our anxiety over the fragility of this peace and all peace will help us to honor this beautiful, fearful hour by casting a thoughtful glance at the world and at ourselves.

These last few years have not been ordinary human years for us; once again we accustomed ourselves to living not human lives but "history," and once again, as after all so-called "great" times, history has left us with a feeling of horror and disgust. How glorious and promising the word "history" sounded in our ears when we were schoolboys, how often as children we yearned to witness and participate in this glamorous history that was known to us only from books and pictures. Bitter experience has taught us that real history is not that of schoolbooks and albums, that it is not a series of great deeds, but an ocean of great sufferings. How tired we are of all the great happenings, the daily flood of news dispatches, the greatest sea, land, and air battles of all time, the whole ghastly competition for world records of horror!

But history is very much like human life in general. Just as we have learned to regard as the best those historical epochs in which history makes itself least noticed, so each of us in his private life has gradually learned to prefer quiet and harmonious times to periods of upheaval, and we appraise the times on the basis not of any philosophy but quite simply of our own personal well-being. Such an attitude is unheroic and banal, but there is something to be said for it: at least it is honest.

Shall we say then that our life is happiest when least is happening, that the world is best off when it has no history but only an existence? Such a notion repels us, it seems so trivial and commonplace; no, we cannot accept it. And from long unvisited chambers of memory there rise to our minds certain verses and maxims of wisdom, such as Goethe's observation that nothing is so hard to bear as a sequence of good days. How sad, when we long so fervently for good days. But Goethe was right: man yearns for happiness but cannot endure too much of it. So it is in the life of the individual: happiness makes him tired and lazy; after a certain time, it ceases to be happiness. Happiness is a lovely flower, but it fades quickly. Perhaps that is also true in history, perhaps the few brief epochs that strike us as well-tempered and enviable must be paid for with the more prevalent misery, blood, and tears.

What then should we wish for if the only choice is between the hell of heroic life and the banality of a life without history?

What should we wish for? That is a question we can ponder a long while without finding an answer. But then it occurs to us that the question is ill-formulated or, rather, that it is a futile, childish question. The long tumult of war seems to have reduced us to a primitive childishness; we have long forgotten what the great teachers of mankind discovered and taught. For thousands of years they have all taught the same thing, and any theologian or humanist can tell us in plain words what it is, regardless of whether he inclines more toward Socrates or toward Lao-tzu, toward the smiling unsuffering Buddha or the Saviour with the crown of thorns. All of them, and indeed every man of insight, every awakened and enlightened one, every true knower and teacher of mankind, has taught this one thing; namely, that man should not wish for greatness or happiness, for heroism or sweet peace, that he should wish for nothing at all but the pure and wakeful mind, the brave heart and faithful, knowing patience that will enable him to endure happiness as well as suffering, tumult as well as silence.

Let us wish for these good gifts. They all have the same source. They come from God, they are nothing other than the divine spark in each one of us. We do not perceive the spark every day; often we go a long time without perceiving it, we forget it, but a single moment can bring it back to us, a moment of terror and despair, or a moment of blissful quietness: a glance into the mystery of a flower, or into the trusting eyes of a child, the sound of a few measures of music. At such moments, moments of extreme affliction or of quiet openness, each one of us knows, even if he cannot say it in words, the secret of all knowledge and all happiness, the secret of unity. The one God lives in us all, every parcel of the earth is our home, every man is our kinsman and brother; that is the knowledge to which we return when dire affliction or sweet rapture opens our ears and makes our hearts capable of love. And this knowledge of divine unity exposes all separation into races, nations, rich and poor, religions and parties as a delusion and a snare.

May this inner peace come to us and to all men: to those who at this hour are going to bed in a secure home and to those who live in misery without home or bed. We wish it to the victors lest their victory make them proud and blind, and to the vanquished lest they inveigh against the suffering that has befallen them and call it down upon the heads of others, in order that they may learn to endure it and to hear the voice of God in it.

Only the handful of saints among men are capable of living for long in this peace and in this good, simple insight; the rest of us are not. This we all know and we have often felt ashamed of it. But once we become aware that the only way to a higher and nobler humanity leads through this forever-repeated experience of unity, through the forever-renewed insight that we men are brothers and of divine origin, once we are truly wounded and awakened by this lightning flash, we shall never be able to fall wholly back to sleep again, and above all we shall not relapse into the nightmarish state of mind which gives rise to wars, racial persecution, and fratricidal strife among men.

Year after year now we have witnessed well-nigh unendurable horror, and others less favored than ourselves have suffered, some here and there are still suffering, every torment of body and soul. Amid blood and tears many have cast off the opinions and classifications by which the average man orders his world in comfortable times. Many have awakened, many have been smitten by conscience, many have sworn: if I live through this, I shall become a different and better man. Today as always these are the *homines bonae voluntatis*, the men of good will; to them a fragment of the world mystery has been disclosed, they alone and not any nations, classes, leagues, or organizations are the repositories of the future, they alone have the secret power of faith.

Once in a sleepless night, sleepless because the atrocities perpetrated under Hitler had just been brought home to me for the first time, I wrote a poem in which I tried, in defiance of the horror, to profess my faith. The last lines of my poem are as follows:

> *Therefore to us erring brothers*
> *Love is possible even in discord.*
> *Not judgment or hatred*
> *But patient love*
> *And loving patience lead*
> *Us closer to the goal.*

Letter to Adele
1946

Dear Adis:

HERE I AM sitting down again to write to you. For your sake and my own, for yours because you are sick, for mine because, in the loneliness—a loneliness that you cannot conceive of—of my life here on our hilltop, I perpetually feel the need to confide in someone who I am sure will not misunderstand me or abuse my confidence. Of course I am not living alone, I have Ninon, my faithful comrade, but sometimes the day is long, like all housewives she has too much to do, and even so I keep her busy every evening playing chess with me or reading to me.

And so I have decided this morning to write to you, to say hello and remind you of the old days. But it is not so easy. I have had no news of you in some time; I only know that you have not been well, that you require care and rest that you cannot have in your home. I don't even know if you are alive, little sister, and even if I knew, I can picture you, but not your life, your apartment, your room, your day. You still have a place to live, for many Germans that in itself is an undreamed-of good fortune, but the apartment is crowded and overrun by visitors, and we here cannot imagine the life you lead there, what you think and talk about. We cannot imagine your joys and sorrows—surely you have both—they are situated in an infinitely remote, alien, dark country, almost on another planet, where joy and sorrow, day and night, life and death have other rules, forms, and meanings than here. The setting of your life is that legendary Germany which until recently we feared for its cruelty and aggressiveness and which today we fear as we might fear a dying or dead neighbor at our door, who carries some unknown fatal disease within him and in his dying seems hardly less terrifying than when he was alive. I know nothing of the objects you live with, of the dresses you wear, the cloth on your table, your cups and saucers; I don't know how close to your windows the horror begins: the demolished houses, the gutted streets and gardens. I don't know what part those terrible, sad things play in your daily life, or to what extent the wounds are healing and covered over by new growth.

And I can't help thinking that you people are no more able to conceive of our life than we of yours. Perhaps you suppose it is rather like your own life before the war, or even before Hitler. The story is that we've been spared, we haven't suffered, we haven't lost anything or made any sacrifices. You and your victorious enemies agree that we little neutrals have been blessed with undeserved good fortune: nothing has happened to us, we had and still have a roof over our heads and our daily bowl of soup. When you think of my village and my house, you no doubt see an island of peace, a little paradise. We ourselves feel impoverished, frustrated, cheated out of the best things of life. In replying to an article in the Swiss press, one of our German friends goes so far as to call us "cookie eaters," and a well-known reeducator of your people has informed me that a man like myself, who spent the Hitler and war periods in sunny, peaceful Tessin, has no claim to a voice in German affairs today. That is quite all right with me, I have never demanded and never will demand a voice in German affairs; but it shows what the world thinks of us. We basked in sunny Tessin and ate cookies, that is its simplistic view of our complex experience of those years. That long before the United States saw fit to draw military consequences from its indignation against Hitler our sons were in uniform year after year; that my whole life work was destroyed by Hitler and by air raids, that my wife's relatives and friends were gassed in Himmler's camps—in the eyes of people hardened by war and misery of all sorts, all that isn't worth mentioning. In short, from whatever angle you look at it, there is a gulf between us and those outside our borders. We have become strangers, we don't understand or even try to understand each other.

The only way I can bridge this terrible gulf and speak to you without restraint or mask is to turn my back on the present and evoke our common possessions and memories. The moment I do that, everything falls into place. Then you are Adis and I am Hermann, I am not a Swiss, you are not a German, there is no borderline and no Hitler between us, even though you cannot visualize my present life nor I yours, all we have to do in the realm of our thousands of memories is to mention the name of a relative, a neighbor, a seamstress, a housemaid, or of a street, a brook, a copse, and the images rise up unmarred, radiating the peace, beauty, and existential force that are no longer present in the frazzled, muddled images of our life since then.

Letter to Adele

Whether my letter reaches you or not, I have already crossed the gap and overcome all estrangement. Now I can speak with you for an hour and remind you and myself of those images which seem to lie so far in the irretrievable past and yet can be conjured up in all their radiance. Though I can only half find you in present-day Germany, in your present home and furnishings, I find you instantly and completely when I think of the house on Müllerweg in Basel and of the horse-chestnut tree in the garden, or of our old house in Calw where we could climb stairway after stairway and find ourselves just under the roof but on a level with the hillside garden, or of the walk to Möttlingen, where our family had close connections dating back to Dr. Barth and the excellent Blumhardt, and of the Sunday mornings in summertime when the two of us on our way there strolled through grain fields sprinkled with cornflowers and poppies, and over stretches of dry heath full of silver thistles and long-stemmed gentians. If you were here and we could talk to one another, you would conjure up a hundred more images of all those places and awaken or refresh a good many of them in me. But even as it is, they are as numberless as the flowers in the meadow. As we take them in and open ourselves to them, the golden legend of our childhood is revived and once more we see before us the world that surrounded us and nurtured us, the world of our parents and ancestors, a world that was both German and Christian, both Swabian and international, a world in which every soul, Christian or not, was held in equal worth and in which neither Jew nor Negro, Hindu nor Chinese was rejected as a stranger. Through the missionary work of our parents and grandparents, our colored

(151

brothers held a special place in our thoughts. We knew a good deal about them and their countries and became acquainted with some of them who stayed with us when they came to Europe. When our grandfathers had visitors from India, either Indians or returning Westerners, we would hear Sanskrit verses and words or phrases in the languages of present-day India. And in our own house, how free the atmosphere was from any suggestion of nationality, let alone nationalism. We had a Swabian grandfather and a French-Swiss grandmother; our father came of a Baltic German family; the eldest of us children, born in India, was an Englishman; the second, who was to complete his studies in Swabia, was a naturalized citizen of Württemberg. The rest of us were citizens of Basel, where our father had acquired citizenship. It was not these circumstances alone that made us permanently incapable of any serious nationalism, but they had a good deal to do with it. It is a good thing for us both that with all the nationalist bluster in the world around us the mere recollection of our childhood and origins makes us immune to such madness. In my eyes you have never been a "German" nor have I ever been a "cookie eater" in yours.

Last summer, with Ninon's help, I prepared another book of my selected poems, the third in twenty-five years. It has been published in an attractive and handy low-priced edition. The page following the title is inscribed: "Dedicated to my sister Adele." You haven't seen it, but perhaps this letter will find its way to you, and then at least you will know that in doing this work, which was also a retrospect of my life, I thought of you and felt your presence beside me. I have also republished my story

Schön ist die Jugend ["Youth, Beautiful Youth"] in a low-priced edition; it is my favorite, and yours too, I believe, among the early stories I wrote in the days before the wars and crises, because it is a very faithful picture of our childhood, of the house where we grew up, and of our home country as it was then. Even so, when I wrote that story I didn't know the world in which we were raised, the world that shaped us, as well as I do now. It was a world of distinctly German and Protestant cast, but with perspectives and ties extending over the entire earth, and it was a whole, harmonious, healthy world, a world without crevices or ghostly veils, a humane and Christian world, into which forest and stream, deer and fox, neighbors and aunts fitted as precisely and organically as Christmas and Easter, Latin and Greek, Goethe, Matthias Claudius and Eichendorff. It was a rich and varied world, but well-ordered; it had a center, and it belonged to us as air and sunshine, rain and wind belonged to us. Who would ever have thought, before war and demons made it plain, that that world would sicken beneath a deadly scab, a leprous semi- reality and unreality, that, beclouded to the point of total alienation, it would be withdrawn from us entirely, leaving us in its stead with the ghostly disorder and insubstantiality of the world as it is today?

But we are able to go back to it, we bear within us an image of a whole, healthy, ordered world and are able to speak with this image—this, and not the fact that we have arms and legs, food to eat and a roof over our heads, is our greatest treasure, our remnant of good fortune. We have something that our children and grandchildren have no longer, or of which they have only a faint glimmer: a divine, noble, beautifully fashioned world in which we can take refuge, in which we who are so estranged from one another in the present can meet and once again know each other completely. Here in the shadow of our ancestors, under the murmuring trees of those days, I come to you, I find you young and gay, and you find me young and whole as I was then. We think of the phlox and cross-of-Jerusalem in our mother's little garden, we think of the fragrant little sandalwood chest and the clouds of pipe smoke in Grandfather's study, and we nod to one another; the calm church steeple rises up before us, and on Sunday morning we see the town musicians on the gallery close to the bells, piping the chorale, a chorale known to us from Gerhardt or Tersteegen or Johann Sebastian Bach. And we think of the "good room" at home, where the tree and the manger are set up on Christmas, and in the music stand we see the old hymnals and song books, Silcher and Schubert, and the piano arrangements of oratorios. And then there was the "other Schubert," the bust, on top of a cupboard in the hallway, of Dr. Gotthilf Heinrich Schubert, author of *The Symbolism of Dreams* and *The History of the Psyche*, who had been a friend of the house. When the weather was bad at Easter and we couldn't go out in the garden, the eggs were hidden in that spacious hallway with its big red sandstone flags, or in the living room with its thousands of books; on the finest eggs little nosegays, grass tassels, and dwarf ferns were to be seen, light against a honey-brown ground. In all these rooms, even after his death, our grandfather's spirit held sway, we thought of him whenever we came home for the holidays. Occasionally we feared him, but we honored and loved him far more: the wise man and magician of India.

waste! Yet I believe that he and his work are no more lost and in vain than any other noble deed or martyr's death amid the horrors of the era of spooks. If anything can cure the world and make mankind pure and whole again, it is the actions and sufferings of those who refused to be bent or bought, who were more willing to lose their lives than their humanity, and these include such warners and teachers as Schrempf, whose life work will not be seen in all its greatness until some later day. Often it seems as though there were nothing real and genuine left in the world, no humanity, no goodness, no truth; but they do exist, and we must not join the ranks of those who have forgotten them.

How beautiful was the September sun on those high holidays of our childhood when we ate plum cake under the chestnut trees and the boys, like Siebenkäs, the advocate of the poor, shot at the wooden eagle! How beautiful were the hidden paths in the tall fir woods, with their ferns and red-flowering foxglove. Sometimes our father stopped by a white fir, scratched a vein with his pocket knife, and gathered a few clear drops of resin in a bottle. He kept this resin to spread on a bruise if the occasion offered, or merely to sniff at. That pure man, who otherwise allowed himself neither indulgence nor vice, was a connoisseur of air and natural fragrance, of oxygen and ozone. I wish I could see his grave again in the Korntal graveyard that used to be so beautiful, but in our situation we had better forgo such wishes.

If I could write the kind of letters our mother used to write, you would learn a good deal about our present life. But I haven't got it in me, and perhaps even our dear mother, that great storyteller, would have fallen silent

(157

today. No, she would have managed, she would have brought order into the chaos of this life and known how to speak of it.

While I have been writing to you, the day has passed, the pale-blue snow looks in at the windows, I have put on the light and now I am as tired as only old people can be.

One should get out of the habit of hoping. Nevertheless, I hope my letter reaches you before too long, and that it is not my last to you.

A Letter to Germany
1946

I<small>T'S</small> <small>STRANGE</small> about letters from your country. For months a letter from Germany was a rare and always joyful event for me. It brought news that a friend I had been worried about, of whom I had long heard nothing, was still alive. And it gave me a glimpse, haphazard and unreliable as it might be, of the country which speaks my language, to which I have entrusted my life work, and which up to a few years ago gave me my bread and the moral justification for my work. Such letters always came as a surprise, were confined to matters of importance and contained no idle chatter; often they were written in great haste while a Red Cross car or a traveler was visiting. Some of them took oddly circuitous routes; a letter written in Hamburg, Halle, or Nuremberg and entrusted to a friendly homeward-bound soldier might reach me months later by way of France or America.

Then the letters became more frequent and longer; a good part of them came from prisoner-of-war camps all over the world, dismal scraps of paper scribbled in the barbed-wire enclosures of Egypt and Syria, in France, Italy, England, or America. Many of these gave me no pleasure at all and I had little desire to answer them. Most of these letters were full of complaints, bitter invective, and sneering criticism of everything under the sun;

they demanded impossible kinds of help and even threatened the world with still another war. There were splendid exceptions but they were few. The rest of the letter writers spoke only of the hard time they were having and complained bitterly of the injustice of their long imprisonment. Not a word about the sufferings which they as German soldiers had for years been inflicting on the world. In reading such letters I was often reminded of a sentence in a German soldier's diary at the time of the invasion of Russia. The author, rather a good fellow in other respects and not really a Nazi, owns that all soldiers were troubled a good deal by the thought of having to die but that having to kill was a purely "tactical" consideration. All these letter writers condemned Hitler; none took any share in the blame.

A prisoner in France, no youngster but already a married man with children, a well-educated industrialist with a university degree, asked me what in my opinion a decent, well-intentioned man should have done in the Hitler period. A man in his position, he argued, could not have prevented anything that happened or opposed Hitler in any way; that would have been madness, it would have cost him his livelihood, his freedom, and in the end his life. I could only reply that the devastation of Russia and Poland, the siege of Stalingrad, and the lunacy of holding it to the bitter end must also have involved certain dangers but that German soldiers had flung themselves into these pursuits with abandon. And why had the German people failed to see through Hitler before 1933? Oughtn't so early an event as the Munich Putsch have shown them what he was? Why, instead of upholding and nurturing the German Republic, the one gratifying consequence of the First World War, had they been almost unanimous in sabotaging it, in voting for Hindenburg and later for Hitler, under whom, to be sure, it became very dangerous to behave like a decent human being? I also reminded such letter writers now and then that the German madness did not begin with Hitler, that the frenzied rejoicing of the people over Austria's vile ultimatum to Serbia in the summer of 1914 might have opened a few eyes. I told them about the struggles and sufferings that Romain Rolland, Stefan Zweig, Frans Masereel, Annette Kolb, and myself endured in those years. But none of them took up the argument, they weren't interested in serious discussion, none of them really wanted to learn or to think.

Then I received a letter from an aged and venerable clergyman in Germany, a pious man who had borne himself very bravely under Hitler and suffered a good deal. He had just read my reflections on the First World War, written twenty-five years ago. As a German and a Christian, he wrote, he was bound to agree with every word I had written. But, to be perfectly sincere, he must also own that if those articles had come to his attention when they were new and timely, he would have thrown them down in indignation, for then, like all good Germans, he had been a staunch patriot and nationalist.

The letters became more and more frequent. Now that regular mail service has been restored in Germany, a small deluge pours in day after day, far more than I have any use for or can possibly read. But though hundreds of people write to me, there are only five or six basic types of letter. Except for the few authentic, personal, and unique documents of these bitter times—and of these few your fine letter was one of the best—all these many letters express certain recurrent and easily recognizable attitudes and needs. Consciously or unconsciously, many of their authors wish to protest their innocence, partly to me, partly to the censorship authorities, and partly to themselves, and undoubtedly not a few of them have good reasons for these exertions.

For instance, there are all the old acquaintances who had written to me for years but stopped when they found out that I was under close surveillance and that corresponding with me could have very unpleasant consequences. Now they inform me that they are still in the land of the living, that they have always thought of me with affection and envied my good fortune at living in the paradise of Switzerland, and that, as I must be well aware, they had never sympathized with those damned Nazis. But many of these old acquaintances were party members for years. Now they tell me how they had one foot in the concentration camp all those years, and I am obliged to reply that the only anti-Nazis I can take seriously are those who had both feet in a camp, not one in a camp and the other in the party. I also remind them that during the war years we expected the Brown devils, our friendly neighbors, to drop into our "Swiss paradise" any minute, and that right here in our paradise the prisons and gallows were waiting for those of us who were on the Black List. At the same time, I have to admit, the reorderers of Europe kept holding out luring bait to us black sheep. At a rather late date, a well-known Swiss colleague amazed me by inviting me to Zürich at "his" expense to discuss my enrollment in the League of European Collaborationists, which had just been founded by Rosenberg's ministry.

Then there are the simple souls, former members of the Youth Movement, who write me that they joined the party about 1934 after a severe inner struggle, for no other purpose than to provide a salutary counterweight to the savage, brutal elements. And so on.

Others have private complexes. They live in utter misery, they have serious worries, and yet they find paper, ink, time, and energy to write me long letters expressing their contempt for Thomas Mann and their indignation that I should be friends with such a man.

Another group consists of former colleagues and friends who openly and unreservedly supported Hitler's triumphal progress all through the years. Now they write me touchingly friendly letters, telling me all about their daily lives, their bomb damage and domestic cares, their children and grandchildren, as though nothing had happened, as though nothing had come between us, as though they had not helped to kill friends and relatives of my wife, who is Jewish, and to discredit and destroy my life work. Not one of them says that he repents, that he sees things in an entirely different light today, that he was deluded. And not one of them says that he was and intends to remain a Nazi, that he regrets nothing, that he stands by his guns. Find me a Nazi who has stood by his guns when things began to go wrong! These people are sickening!

A few of the letter writers expect me to switch my allegiance to Germany, to come back and help to reeducate the people. A good many more call on me to raise my voice in the outside world, to protest as a neutral and humanitarian against the commissions or omissions of the occupying powers. How can they be so naïve, so utterly ignorant of the world and the times, so touchingly, embarrassingly childish!

Probably all this infantile or malignant absurdity doesn't even surprise you, probably you have seen more of it than I. You intimate that you have written me a long letter about the state of mind in your unfortunate country but because of the censorship have not sent it. Well, I have tried to give you an idea of what takes up the greater part of my days and hours, partly by way of explaining why I am publishing this letter. Obviously I cannot answer the mass of letters I receive, most of which demand and expect the impossible of me; yet some of them, I felt, should not be ignored. To their authors I address this published letter, if only because they inquire so kindly about my well-being.

Your welcome letter belongs to none of the categories I have mentioned; it contains not a single stereotyped phrase and—a miracle in present-day Germany!—not a single word of complaint or accusation. Your good, intelligent, kind letter has done me a world of good, and what it says of your own life has moved me deeply. So you too, like our faithful friend, were long watched and spied on, thrown into the prisons of the Gestapo, and even condemned to death! I was horrified to hear of all this, especially as my letters, for all my precaution, must have been one more mark against you, but your news did not really surprise me. For I never thought of you as having one foot in a prison or camp and the other in the party; I never doubted that you would be brave and alert as befits your clear eyes and intelligence, or that you were on the right side. So it was obvious that you would be in serious danger.

You see, I haven't much to say to most of my German correspondents. Certain things are very much the same as at the end of the First World War, and besides, I have grown older and more suspicious. Just as today all my German friends are united in their condemnation of Hitler, so then, in the early days of the German Republic, they were united in condemning militarism, war, and violence. They all fraternized, a little late but very effusively, with us opponents of the war; Gandhi and Rolland were revered almost as saints. The slogan of the day was *"Nie wieder Krieg!"* ("No more war!"). But only a few years later Hitler was able to risk his Munich Putsch. Accordingly, I cannot take very seriously the present unanimity in condemning Hitler; to my mind it offers not the slightest guarantee of a political change of heart, or even of a political insight. I do, however, take seriously, very seriously, the change of heart, the purification and maturity of those individuals who amid the vast affliction, the burning martyrdom of these years, have found the way inward, the way to the heart of the world, who have learned to look into the timeless reality of life. These Awakened Ones have sensed and experienced and suffered the great mystery very much as I experienced it in the bitter years after 1914, except that they have done so under far greater pressure, amid more cruel sufferings, and undoubtedly countless men have collapsed and succumbed on the way to this experience and this awakening, before they could mature.

Behind the barbed wire of a prisoner-of-war camp in Africa a German captain writes to me of recollections of Dostoevsky's *House of the Dead* and of *Siddhartha,* and tells me how, in the midst of a pitiless life which leaves no room for a moment's solitude, he is trying to find the way of meditation and to penetrate to the core of things, though he has "not definitely decided to withdraw from the surface manifestations of life." A woman, formerly imprisoned by the Gestapo, writes: "Prison has taught me a great deal and the worries of day-to-day life no longer oppress me." These are positive experiences, marks of real life, and I could cite many more such statements if I had the time and eyesight to reread all these letters.

You ask me how I am getting along; the question is quickly answered. I have grown old and tired, and the destruction of my work, begun by Hitler's ministries and completed by American bombs, has given my last years a ground bass of disillusionment and sorrow. My consolation is that an occasional little melody rises above the ground bass, and that there are still hours when I am able to dwell in the timeless. In order that some part of my work may survive, I prepare from time to time a Swiss reprint of some book that has been unavailable for years; it is not much more than a gesture, because of course these reprints are obtainable only in Switzerland.

Old age brings sclerosis, and sometimes my blood refuses to irrigate my brain properly. But, after all, these evils have their good side: one doesn't react to things so violently, one disregards a good deal, one becomes immune to certain blows and pinpricks, and a part of the being that was once I has already gone where the whole of it will soon be.

Among the good things which I am *still* able to enjoy, which still give me pleasure and compensate for the dark side, are the rare but undeniable indications that an authentic spiritual Germany lives on. I neither seek nor find them in the bustlings of its present culture-manufacturers and fair-weather democrats but in such gratifying manifestations of determination, alertness, and courage, of good will and of confidence shorn of illusions, as your letter. I thank you for it. Preserve the seed, keep faith with the light and the spirit. There are very few of you, but you may be the salt of the earth.

Message to the
Nobel Prize Banquet
1946

I N TENDERING my heartfelt and respectful greetings, I
wish first of all to express my regret that I cannot
be your guest, that I am unable to greet you and thank
you in person. My health has always been poor and the
hardships of the National Socialist period, during which
my life work was destroyed in Germany and I was bur-
dened day after day with arduous duties, undermined it
for good. Still, my spirit is unbroken and I feel very much
at one with you in the idea underlying the Nobel Foundation, the idea that culture is supranational and international, and under obligation to serve not war and destruction but peace and reconciliation. In honoring me with
the Nobel Prize, you have at the same time honored the
German language and the German contribution to world
culture. In this I see a gesture of conciliation and good
will, a move to restore and enlarge cultural cooperation
among peoples.

But my ideal is not a cultural uniformity in which national characteristics are blurred. By no means. I am all
in favor of diversity, differentiation, and gradation on our
beloved earth! It is a wonderful thing that there should
be many races and nations, many languages, many varia-

tions in mentality and outlook. If I hate and am irreconcilably opposed to war, conquests, and annexations, it is in part because they destroy so much of the historically determined individuality and differentiation of human culture. I am an enemy of the *"grands simplificateurs"* and a lover of equality, of organic form, of the inimitable. And so, as your grateful guest and colleague, I hold out my hand to your country, to Sweden, with its language and culture, its rich, proud history, and the energy with which it has preserved and developed its national character.

I have never been in Sweden, but over the years quite a few welcome tokens of friendship have come to me from your country. The first, which I received some forty years ago, was a Swedish book, the first edition of *Christ Legends* with an inscription in the hand of Selma Lagerlöf. Over the years I have had a number of valuable exchanges with your country, culminating in this last great gift it has surprised me with. I give it my profound thanks.

Words of Moralizing Thanks
1946

WITH THESE LINES I wish to thank those who have congratulated me on the occasion of the Goethe Prize. My feelings and thoughts on receiving these congratulations were so contradictory that it has been hard for me to express them even in part. I ask my friends to receive the result with indulgence.

Some of you are no doubt surprised or even displeased that I have accepted this honor, and to tell you the truth my first purely instinctive reaction was not yes but no. My unconscious reaction sprang from such considerations as these: Acceptance would put a considerable strain on an already overburdened old man. Moreover, it would look like a kind of reconciliation with official Germany. And it would be grotesque and intrinsically false to accept this prize as a kind of retribution or settlement from a country whose bankruptcy I fully share for the second time, a country to which I entrusted my life work and which destroyed it. No, I said to myself on this first impulse, what I might reasonably expect and demand of Germany is my simple right, my rehabilitation from the dishonor thrown on me by Goebbels and Rosenberg, the restoration of my work or at least a part of it, and, what would seem only too simple and obvious, financial compensation for my work. But the Germany in whose power it would be to grant me that exists no longer. And how thorny and complex, how double-edged and difficult the relations between this great, puzzling, capricious people and myself since the First World War! Only a few days before I had to decide whether or not to accept the prize, another pile of insulting letters came to me from Germany, and all in all they struck me as an adequate expression of the relationship between me and this people whose language has been my instrument and spiritual home and whose political behavior in the world I had looked on with increasing disapproval since 1914 and often enough commented on.

But no sooner had I begun to think about these first reactions than equally good arguments on the other side presented themselves. The prize was not offered to me by that "Germany" which existed no longer but by the good old staunchly democratic city of Frankfurt with its markedly Jewish culture, a city which the Hohenzollerns had so thoroughly detested ever since the meetings in St. Paul's Church, and by a committee which behaved honorably and with real courage under the pressure of the Hitler period and which was assuredly well aware that in selecting me it would make enemies of the group among whom my hate-ridden letters originated, the fanatical nationalists who have been momentarily defeated but have by no means vanished from the world.

Of course I could not have accepted the prize if it had involved any material advantage to myself. But this is not the case; the money will stay in Germany and is to be given away.

Prizes and honors are not exactly what they seem to us in our early years. For the beneficiary they are neither a pleasure nor a festive occasion, nor a merited reward. They are a small component of the complex phenomenon —resulting largely from misunderstandings—which is known as fame, and should be accepted for what they are: attempts on the part of the official world to overcome its embarrassment in the presence of unofficial achievements. On both sides they are a symbolic gesture, an expression of good breeding and manners.

The fact that this prize is named after Goethe makes it impossible for the receiver to feel worthy of it. It is unlikely that many of the previous prize-winners felt worthy of it. We children of a calamitous epoch cannot put ourselves on a plane either with Goethe the poet or with Goethe the man. Nevertheless, I recall with a smile certain of his observations on the character of the Germans, and sometimes it seems to me that if Goethe were our contemporary he would more or less agree with my diagnosis of the two great ailments of our day. For in my opinion the present state of mankind springs from two mental disorders: the megalomania of technology and the megalomania of nationalism. It is they that give the present-day world its face and its image of itself. They have been responsible for two world wars and their consequences, and before their fury is spent they will have further similar consequences.

Resistance to these two world ailments is today the most important task and justification of the human spirit. To this resistance I have devoted my life, a ripple in the stream.

So much for the moral aspect. To us old people, especially when we are in a bad way, the world is primarily a moral phenomenon and problem, its face is gruesome to gloomy. But a child, a pious believer in God, a poet or philosopher sees a very different world, a world with a thousand faces, some of them infinitely appealing. And if today, availing myself of the customary privilege of the aged, I moralize a bit, I beg you not to forget that tomorrow or the day after, on this side or the other side of the grave, I shall probably be a poet, a pious believer, or a child again, and the world and history will no longer strike me as a moral problem but once more as an eternal divine drama and picture book.

And perhaps when it has fully renounced its active, leading role, our deathly sick Europe will be restored to its former high estate and become once more a quiet reservoir, a treasure of noblest memories, a haven of souls in roughly the same sense as my friends today attach to the magic word "Orient."

To a Young Colleague in Japan
1947

Dear Colleague:

YOUR LONG LETTER of January, which reached me
at cherry-blossom time, was the first word of greeting to find its way to me from your country after years of
silence. And I can see by a number of indications that, as
you say, your message of greeting and sympathy comes to
me from a violently shaken world, a world that has seemingly fallen back into chaos. In my country, the envied
"island of peace," you hope to find a still intact world of
the spirit, an accepted and valid hierarchy of values. In a
way you are right. Your passionate letter, animated at
once by faith and by anguish, was written amid the ruins
of a big city where it was difficult even to procure paper
and envelope. Delivered by a friendly country post-
woman, it arrived here amid the peace of an undestroyed
house and village, at a time when our whole valley is
flooded with cherry blossoms and the cuckoo can be
heard all day. And since your letter is that of a young
man to an old man, it comes to a place where, in a spiritual sense as well, there is no chaos but a certain order
and stability. This order and stability, however, are not a
product of the general situation in the Western world, of
a more or less well-preserved heritage of faith and custom; they spring rather from a tradition which lives on

amid chaos in the insular existence of an individual. Here in this country there are many such individuals, old people with a decent cultural background, and by and large they are not persecuted or even despised and ridiculed; on the contrary, they are respected, their fellow citizens take pleasure in them and preserve them amid the twilight of values, just as they preserve dying animal species in national parks; occasionally they even take pride in us and hold us up as a purely Western heritage, not to be found in such rising new countries as Russia and the United States. But we old poets, thinkers, and believers are no longer the head or heart of the Western world, we are vestiges of a dying race, taken seriously at most by ourselves; we have no progeny.

And now to your letter. You speak of concerns that strike me as superfluous. You express a certain indignation that your fellow students do not, like you, regard me as a hero and martyr to truth but only as a minor sentimental writer from south Germany. Both you and they are right and wrong; there is no point in taking such formulations seriously. Or rather: there is no point in correcting your comrades' judgment of me, for whether right or wrong their judgment harms no one. On the other hand, dear colleague, your own judgment and evaluation of me does call for scrutiny and correction because it might do harm. You are not merely a young reader who in a particularly receptive moment has laid hands on a few books which he loves, to which he is grateful, which he esteems and overestimates. That is the right of every reader, every reader is perfectly entitled to worship or despise a book; that can do no harm. But you are not merely an enthusiastic young reader; you are, as you tell

me, a young colleague of mine, a writer at the beginning
of his career, a young man who loves the true and the
beautiful and feels called upon to bring light and truth to
men. And in my opinion what is permissible for a naïve
reader is not permissible for a budding writer, a man who
is himself going to write and publish books: he has no
right to worship uncritically the books and authors that
happen to impress him, let alone take them as models. Of
course your love of my books is not a sin, but it is uncriti-
cal and immoderate and consequently can do you little
good as a writer. You see in me what you yourself hope to
become, you think I am worth imitating and emulating:
you see in me a champion of truth, a hero and torch-
bearer, a God-inspired bringer of light if not the light
itself. And that, as you will soon see, is not only an exag-
geration and boyish idealization; it is a fundamental error.
Let the naïve reader, to whom books do not mean so
much, think what he likes of the writer, it doesn't matter;
whatever he says will be idle talk, it's as if a man who
would never as long as he lived build so much as a wood-
shed were to expound his opinions on architecture. But a
young writer passionately in love with his favorite authors, full of idealism and unconsciously, no doubt, of
ambition as well, who conceives radically wrong ideas
about books and literature, is not harmless; he is dangerous, he can do harm and above all he can harm himself.
That is why I am answering your kind and moving letter
not with a friendly picture postcard but with these lines.
As a future writer you have a responsibility to yourself
and your future readers.

The hero and bringer of light that you see in your favorite author of the moment and that you yourself hope to

become is a figure I don't care for. It's too pretty, too empty, too high-flown, and above all it's too Occidental to have grown on your own Eastern soil.

The author who has awakened you or given you an insight is neither a light nor a torch-bearer; he is at best a window through which light can shine on the reader. His distinction has nothing whatever to do with heroism, noble intentions, or ideal programs; his only function is that of a window: not to stand in the way of the light but to let the light through. Possibly he will long to do noble deeds, to become a benefactor of mankind, and just as possibly such a longing will be his ruin, preventing him from admitting the light. He must not be guided and spurred on by pride or by a frantic striving for humility but solely by love of light, by openness to reality and truth.

It should not be necessary to remind you of this, for you are neither a savage nor a victim of faulty education but an adherent of Zen Buddhism. Thus you have a faith, you have the guidance of a spiritual discipline that has few equals in teaching men to admit the light, to open themselves to the truth. This guidance will carry you farther than any of our Western books, some of which hold such magic for you now. I have great respect for Zen, far more than for your rather European-tinged ideals. Zen, as you know better than I, is a wonderful school of the mind and heart; here in the West we have few comparable traditions, and they are not so well preserved. We have a rather strange way of looking at each other, you and I, a young Japanese and an elderly European; we both feel sympathy, neither of us is immune to a certain exotic charm in the other, each of us suspects that the other possesses something which he himself cannot fully attain. Your Zen, I feel confident, will protect you against such exoticism and false idealism, just as the good school of classical antiquity and Christianity forbids me to turn my back, in despair at our spiritual situation, on the tradition that has thus far sustained me and to throw myself into the arms of some Indian or other system of Yoga. For at times, I cannot deny, there is such a temptation. But, despite all the magic of Oriental disciplines, my European education teaches me to distrust those aspects of them that I do not understand or only half understand and to confine myself to that part of them which I have really succeeded in understanding. And that part is closely related to the teachings and experience of my own spiritual home.

Buddhism in the form of Zen, the form in which you know it, will be your guide and support as long as you live. It will help you to keep from being submerged in the chaos that has broken over the world. But some time it may bring you into conflict with your literary plans. Literature is a dangerous occupation for a man with a good religious education. A writer must believe in the light, he must know it through incontrovertible experience and must be as wide open to it as possible, but he must not regard himself as a bringer of light and surely not as the light itself. For, if he does, the window will close and the light, which does not need us, will go other ways.

(Postscript, a few days later)

A package of printed matter that I sent you the other day and the original of this letter have just been returned by the post office as unacceptable. What a strange world we are living in! You, an inhabitant of a defeated country occupied by the victor, have been able to send me an eighteen-page letter; I, a mere inhabitant of a neutral country, am not permitted to answer you. But perhaps this greeting will reach you one day through the newspaper.

An Attempt at Justification
TWO LETTERS CONCERNING PALESTINE

Genoa, May 22, 1948

Dear Herr Hesse:

BEFORE BOARDING THE SHIP that will take me back to my home in Haifa, I wish to make a request of you:

If only you, either alone or in conjunction with other world-famous writers, might raise your voice in this tragic hour in Jewish history! The invasion, which is setting the torch to what the selfless and unstinting toil of generations has created—the settlements, those true islands of human purity, the cities with their populations and libraries—is not only threatening sites dear to all mankind—it will also, if the civilized world does not soon intervene, destroy the incunabula and manuscripts in Jerusalem and Tel Aviv, among them, to give only two examples, the entire unpublished work of Novalis and Franz Kafka, in addition to the most magnificent pictures, scientific and artistic collections. The intellectuals of all nations should make an extreme effort to prevent this from happening and to restore peace.

I am convinced that your voice will go far toward arousing the conscience of mankind from its deep sleep.

MAX BROD

An Attempt at Justification

Montagnola, May 25, 1948

Dear Herr Brod:

ALMOST EVERY DAY the mails bring me a handful of requests, mostly from Germany. Someone is ill and ought to be in a sanatorium where he will receive proper care. Someone is a writer, scientist, or artist, he has been sharing a single room with three or four other people for years and hasn't even got a table; if he is to be saved, he must be provided, if only for a short time, with peace and quiet and working space. "At the merest hint from you, the social-service agencies will spring into action," writes one. And another: "A word from you to the Swiss authorities will suffice to get the poor man an entry visa and working permit, perhaps even the right to apply for citizenship." In reply to all these letters I can only say that in our country a hint from me will move neither the authorities nor any other institution, neither a sanatorium nor even a bakery shop to give a hungry man, regardless of who he may be, so much as a meal. I am amazed and saddened by these petitioners' childlike belief in a magician who need only lift his finger to turn misery into happiness or war into peace.

And now you, the old friend of the profoundly tragic Kafka, turn to me in a similar matter, and this time I am to assist not one or several individuals but an entire people, and help "to restore peace" in the bargain. The whole idea horrifies me, for I must confess that I have no faith whatever in the concerted action of intellectuals or in the good will of the "civilized world." The mind cannot be measured in terms of quantity, and whether ten or a hundred "leading lights" appeal to the mighty to do or not

(181

do something, such an appeal is equally hopeless. If years ago you had addressed an appeal for humanity, piety, and nonviolence to the young terrorist groups in your own nation, they would have told you in no uncertain terms what armed activists think of such ideals.

No, noble as your intention is, I cannot share your attitude. On the contrary, I regard every "spiritual" pseudo-action, every plea, sermon, or threat addressed by intellectuals to the lords of the earth, as false, as harmful and demeaning to the spirit, as something to be avoided under all circumstances. Our kingdom, my dear Max Brod, is simply "not of this world." Our business is not to preach or to command or to plead but to stand fast amid hells and devils. We cannot expect to exert the least influence through our fame or through the concerted action of the greatest possible number of our fellows. In the long view, to be sure, we shall always be the winners, something of us will remain when all the ministers and generals of today have been forgotten. But in the short view, in the here and now, we are poor devils, and the world wouldn't dream of letting us join in its game. If we poets and thinkers are of any importance, it is solely because we are human beings, because for all our failings we have hearts and minds and a brotherly understanding of everything that is natural and organic. The power of the ministers and other policy-makers is based not on heart or mind but on the masses whose "representatives" they are. They operate with something that we neither can nor should operate with, with number, with quantity, and that is a field we must leave to them. They too have no easy time of it, we must not forget that, actually they are worse off than we are, because they have not an intelligence, a rest and unrest, an equilibrium of their own, but are carried along, buffeted, and in the end wiped away by the millions of their electorate. Nor are they unmoved by the hideous things that go on under their eyes and partly as a result of their mistakes; they are very much bewildered. They have their house rules that cover them and perhaps make their responsibility more bearable. We guardians of the spiritual substance, we servants of the word and of truth, watch them with as much pity as horror. But our house rules, we believe, are more than house rules, they are true commandments, eternal and divine laws. Our mission is to safeguard them, and we endanger that mission with every compromise; we endanger it every time we agree, even with the noblest intentions, to play by their "rules."

This blunt statement, I know, will lead certain superficial thinkers to suspect me of being one of those dreamy artists who believe that art has nothing to do with politics, that an artist must live in an aesthetic ivory tower for fear of corrupting his vision by contact with crude reality, or soiling his hands. I know that to you I have no need to defend myself in this respect. Since the First World War awakened me inexorably to reality, I have many times raised my voice and have devoted a large part of my life to the responsibility that was then borne in on me. But I have always strictly observed limits: as a writer I have time and time again reminded my readers of the fundamental commandments of humanity, but I myself have never attempted to exert an influence on policy, I have never set hand to any of the hundreds of solemn but fruitless proclamations, protests, and cries of warning that our intellectuals keep issuing to the detriment of the humanitarian cause. And I have no intention of doing so.

Though I have not been able to comply with your request, I have, as you see, done my best to pass it on to others by publishing your letter and my answer.

Yours,
HERMANN HESSE

On Romain Rolland
1948

W E KNOW THE PART played by Leo Tolstoy in the
early development of Romain Rolland. The boy's
letter to the old man was taken seriously and answered;
the famous man replied earnestly and lovingly to the
schoolboy's questions, he responded like a father and a
brother to the troubled child's impetuous outpouring. In
so doing, the venerable sage performed a sacred and
magical act, the act of transmitting a calling. And in the
course of his rich and fruitful life, Rolland was to perform
this same act a number of times. As an older man who
had found his way, he encouraged younger men who
were searching and, once he was convinced of their good
will, transmitted the call to them. As an awakener, an
adviser, a comrade in struggle, he was helpful to the
earnest seekers of his own generation and the two suc-
ceeding generations. He guarded a flame that is not yet
extinguished, not even in Germany, where during the
days of terror his forbidden books sharpened the eyesight
and conscience, and sustained the hearts, of a faithful
few. I still receive reminders of Rolland from Germany, I

Written at the end of 1948 for a Rolland memorial program on
the Paris radio.

am questioned about my personal memories of him and asked for his books.

Dispersed throughout the world, there are many pious believers outside the churches and denominations, men of good will who are gravely alarmed at the decline of the human spirit, at the wasting away of peace and confidence in the world. These men have no priests, no ecclesiastical consolations, but they too have their voices crying out in the wilderness, their saints and martyrs. Among these were Romain Rolland; Leo Tolstoy, his awakener; and Mahatma Gandhi, his comrade and friend. Those three great consolers are dead but they live on in thousands of hearts; they help thousands to keep faith and to hold up their light to the sluggish unreasoning world.